P9-BXY-479

PIE
OME
TRY

PIE OME TRY

MODERN TART ART AND PIE DESIGN
FOR THE EYE AND THE PALATE

LAUREN KO

WILLIAM MORROW

An Imprint of HarperCollins*Publishers*

TO ALL THE OTHER REGULAR
NOBODIES OUT THERE MINDING THEIR
OWN BUSINESS, DREAMING DREAMS
THEY DON'T EVEN KNOW THEY HAVE . . .
YOU NEVER KNOW WHERE LIFE WILL
TAKE YOU AND WHAT MAGIC AWAITS.
THIS IS FOR YOU.

AND ABOVE ALL,
WATCH WITH GLITTERING EYES
THE WHOLE WORLD AROUND YOU
BECAUSE THE GREATEST SECRETS ARE
ALWAYS HIDING IN THE MOST UNLIKELY
PLACES. THOSE WHO DON'T BELIEVE
IN MAGIC WILL NEVER FIND IT.
—ROALD DAHL

CONTENTS

HAPPY AS A GRAM   51
Cranberry curd with a speculoos crust and kiwi, mango, and dragon fruit

OF A SHINGLE MIND   55
Honey ricotta tart with an herbed pastry shell and beets

SWIM WITH THE SPARKS   59
Blood orange chipotle curd with a buttery pastry shell and mango

STICKS OF THE TRADE   62
Lemongrass grapefruit curd with a buttery pastry shell and pineapple

RIGHTS OF FANCY   65
Hong Kong–style egg custard with a matcha pastry shell and strawberry

LIFE OF THE TARTY   68
Lemon basil curd with a buttery pastry shell and kiwi

TILE BY FIRE   71
Passion fruit curd with a speculoos crust and papaya

TRUTH OR SQUARE   75
Mint chip ice cream with a funfetti Oreo crust and Andes mints

MOST VALUABLE LAYER   78
No-bake matcha white chocolate cheesecake with a matcha pastry shell and coconut and chocolate

HEX AND BALANCES   81
Spirulina lemon curd with a coconut pecan crust and papaya and pink dragon fruit

LIVIN' ON A PAIR   86
Swirled lemon curds with a coconut pecan crust and kiwi and dragon fruit

BERRIED TREASURE   89
Lavender blackberry whipped cream with a shortbread crust and berries

HEADS OR SCALES   92
Blueberry mint curd with a speculoos crust and kiwi

THE SECRET INGRADIENT   95
Black sesame white chocolate mousse with a matcha pastry shell and cherries

PLAY TO FIN   98
Sweet cream with a chocolate matcha shortbread crust and plums

NO RINGS ATTACHED   103
Smoked salmon cream with an everything (but the) bagel pastry shell and heirloom tomatoes

WAVE OF WONDERS   105
Cardamom coffee cream with a shortbread crust and pear

JEWEL'S PARADISE   109
Gingerbread caramel cream with a shortbread crust and fig and pomegranate

SURVIVAL OF THE KNITTEST   113
Peanut butter mousse with a funfetti Oreo crust and apple

SPIKE A POSE   117
Black tea panna cotta with a buttery pastry shell and strawberry and mango

A MARBLE TO BEHOLD   119
Caramelized onion and potato with an herbed pastry shell and Irish Porter Cheddar

THE FIG IS UP   122
Chocolate hazelnut ganache with a chocolate pastry shell and fig

PIES

INTRODUCTION

WHEN ALL HELL BAKES LOOSE

Having flown in on a turbulent redeye that morning, I hadn't slept in nearly thirty hours and was seeing stars. Literally. I was elbows deep in flour and totally overwhelmed by a fancy test kitchen full of equipment I didn't know how to use when Martha Stewart sauntered by.

"Oh! You're the crazy pie lady! Your work is beautiful!" If I was barely functional before, I was definitely dead now. Was this real life?

She continued, "I'm really looking forward to learning from you. I have not been able to figure out how you construct your intricate designs! I can't wait!" Then she floated on, leaving me stuttering in her wake.

Seriously, though. I'm a self-taught, hobbyist home baker who stumbled into pie baking because I was unemployed and bored of making blueberry muffins. I made my first pie in late 2016, and I started with a cracked pie plate, a small paring knife, and a cookie sheet.

A few months later, preparing to bake in the presence of a culinary icon, I still hadn't made many upgrades. I mean, I now had a ruler and a pastry wheel, both of which were the cheapest versions I could source online, and I had graduated to disposable foil pie tins. Things couldn't have been more snoring and understated if I tried.

So how does a regular person like me even end up here—as a social media personality with a cult following—in New York, trying not to pass out from fatigue and shock?

HERE WE DOUGH, FROM THE BEGINNING.

I hail from a family of phenomenal eaters. The kind of insane people who sit down to a casual eight-course lunch and, before even taking their first bite, begin to discuss plans for dinner. I heartily ate my way through childhood, surrounded by gourmet home cooks and snack enthusiasts alike. I was immersed in equal parts fragrant seafood paella and Flamin' Hot Cheetos. There were both glossy caramel flans and boxed brownie mixes.

I could assemble shrimp ceviche in my sleep and bake off dozens of chewy chocolate chip cookies, and I even made my own wedding cake.

But pie? Nope. Too scary. Too much work. In fact, I don't have any recollection of anyone in my family ever making a pie. We left that to Marie Callender.

So fall of 2016 rolls around. I'm newly settled in Seattle, with a surplus of free time as I prowl for a job. And to really drive home the point that I had no professional kitchen experience whatsoever, I was a social worker turned nonprofit executive assistant. How about that eight-to-five office grind?

One night while blooping around on the Internet, I stumbled across some beautiful photographs of pies on Pinterest. The pies were layered with floral and foliage cutouts, and they stunned me with their detailed charm. Spellbound by the prospect of using pie as an art medium, I suddenly wondered if I too could master pie. Determined to overcome my (unfounded, as it turns out) anxiety toward pie dough, I set out to conquer my fear. But the romantic, feminine aesthetic of bakers like Julie Jones and Jo Harrington wasn't for me, and the only decorative implement I had on hand anyway was a giant T-Rex cookie cutter. So, by default—straight lines. A simple plaid lattice apple pie was my first attempt and it was fine.

A month later, I made my second pie and brought it to Thanksgiving dinner at my in-laws' house. I was so proud of the intricate grid pattern I had painstakingly crafted out of dough on top. Horrifyingly, the inside was a runny disaster. The marionberry filling was overly juicy and the bottom crust completely undercooked. The back seat of our car looked like a gruesome crime scene. My husband's wonderful parents kindly insisted on eating their slices as I sat by mortified. That was the end of my pie pilgrimage.

Or so I thought.

Fast forward a year, to August 29, 2017, when, worried that I was becoming *that* friend who was flooding her personal Instagram account with food photos (Here's me on a hike! Here are seven galettes and a summer salad. Here's my dog! Here are five hundred pies!), I started a separate account, @lokokitchen. Intending to use it just as a holding place for pictures of the food I was making, I began with about one hundred followers—my husband, my baby cousin, and a few people from high school I hadn't talked to in years.

Thanks to an obnoxious abundance of summer produce and an ambitious orchard trip that saw me home with ten pounds of cherries, I found myself baking pies anew. I had tired of muffins again and was now far enough removed from the trauma of Pie-saster 2016 to attempt a return to pastry. At the very least, it was an excellent way to use up large quantities of fruit. My first Lokokitchen Instagram post was a peach pie with an abstract geometric design I carved using my paring knife, with a cookie sheet as a straight-edge guide. My technique was unwieldy and impractical, but I didn't know any better, and I was quite pleased with the result. Six hundred people on the Internet were, too. *What.* Cue the shock.

Over the subsequent weeks, I continued to post pictures of my baking forays. I used my older-generation iPhone to take photographs and a ten-dollar chalkboard from Home Depot as my backdrop. Much to my bewilderment, I gained followers steadily—strangers I didn't know from anywhere who

were apparently interested in my pies. Then I published a photo of a blueberry pie with what has now become my signature spoke design (Spoke Signals; page 205). I hit 1,000 followers, and my brain exploded.

A month after that, Design Milk reposted one of my photos to their Instagram account, and I skyrocketed to more than 12,000 followers, gaining 8,000 in one day. I hadn't even heard of Design Milk before that point, but they had an audience of 1 million people, and the exposure launched me fully into the public eye.

It was the beginning of all hell baking loose—the insanity otherwise known as "going viral." From there, outlets like Food52, O magazine, BuzzFeed, and Vogue shared my photos on their platforms and wrote features about my unusual style. People everywhere responded overwhelmingly, and things continued to snowball.

Over the next year, I proceeded to make and share my pies and tarts, racking up more than 200,000 followers. Local and international news agencies reached out for interviews. Large social media accounts promoted my content on their platforms. BuzzFeed Tasty brought me into their studio to film, and the video immediately trended in the top 10 on YouTube, hitting 12 million views on Facebook within a week. I started holding workshops in Seattle and flying to events around the country. I quit my full-time office job, if only to dig myself out of the enormous email cavern of people imploring me to sell pies, and to reclaim my weekends, which had become marathon baking sessions.

Not even pairing a pie photo with a caption about pooping my pants as an adult (twice!) deterred people from following my baking adventures.

SO HERE WE ARE.

There is a shroud of mystery surrounding my pie art, since I haven't widely shared my techniques or recipes, and the general impression is that one must be both a world-renowned pastry chef and a theoretical mathematician to execute the designs. Let's be clear—I am neither. I am simply a humble nerd puttering around in her home kitchen.

Despite a lack of professional culinary, pastry, or design training, and the fact that I've always been miserable at math, I've spawned an entire movement of modern geometric pie design around the world. All this is to really say, I've somehow managed to trick millions of eyeballs into thinking that I perform some sort of otherworldly sorcery with dough as my medium and insanity as my muse.

But now the secret's out. My techniques are straightforward and far easier than you think. You don't need wizard wands or expensive butter made from the milk of royal cows in the hinterlands. Just time, patience, and a bit of crumbtion.

I'm that lady who couldn't figure out how to fit the lid on the food processor in Martha Stewart's kitchen. Also, I failed calculus. But I can make geometric pie art, and so can you. Whether you're a seasoned food professional, a curious home baker, or an enthusiastic eater, there's a slice for everyone. Let's get this tarty started.

ROLL UP THOSE SLEEVES.

This book is organized into two parts: Tarts and Pies. Each section starts with a compendium of crust and dough recipes, which can often be mixed and matched with other fillings within its tart or pie grouping. Designs can also be implemented interchangeably. I provide recommendations on alternate pairings and substitutions after each design tutorial, but ultimately, this book is structured with the hope that you will make these creations entirely your own. Experiment with crust, filling, and design medleys. Play with colors and flavors. Dive headlong into this pie life for yourself. I can't wait to see where it takes you!

If you're new to baking or pie design, Truth or Square (page 75) or Mother of Swirl (page 181) make solid first forays. They're surefire bets for getting your feet wet before venturing into the deep end with more complicated undertakings, like Seeing Is Beweaving (page 247).

EQUIPMENT

When I made my first pie in 2016, I had just moved across the country into a tiny apartment in Seattle and was still settling in. I didn't even have a ruler to my name, so I cut dough strips with a baking sheet and a not-sharp-enough knife. It was unwieldy, but as a pie-baking novice, I couldn't justify purchasing an arsenal of fancy equipment to explore what I saw as a one-off venture (ha!). Besides, I didn't even know there was such a thing as a pastry wheel, and in any case, priority was directed to more crucial items like . . . oh, a mattress. Even now that my life is completely consumed by pie and my house is more than filled with all sorts of gadgets, my core baking toolkit remains fairly basic.

Furthermore, while quality is important, practically speaking, I generally seek out the most economical versions when purchasing equipment. None of these items requires the "splurge model," and in fact, I encourage you to look around your kitchen and repurpose what you have whenever possible.

This is not a comprehensive list of tools used in this book. These are simply the essentials that bear mentioning.

BAKING SHEETS (FLAT AND RIMMED): Flat (unrimmed) baking sheets are supremely useful for sliding under rolled-out pie dough when the whole operation needs to cool down in the fridge. Since the supreme law of pie land is *keep things cold*, the ability to chill your dough quickly at any point of the design process is crucial. Rimmed baking sheets are equally important for catching bubbling juices when baking pies. Unless smoking out your house and spending hours scrubbing blackened puddles on the bottom of your oven happen to be your ideal weekend pastimes, I recommend setting all your pie and tart pans on a rimmed sheet before baking.

BAKING WEIGHTS: Unless you already own a set, there is no need to purchase specifically marketed pie weights. Dried goods like beans, rice, or, as extolled by pastry wizard Stella Parks, even sugar, set in foil serve the purpose perfectly well and are pleasantly affordable. At some point, I amassed a quantity of pearl barley beyond anything I could sanely consume, so I keep the grains in a large container and reuse them exclusively as baking weights.

BENCH SCRAPER: Not only is this tool handy for cleanly dividing double batches of pie dough, it also makes clearing off crusty debris from your work surface a breeze.

CRUST SHIELD: Pie edges often brown before the fillings are cooked through, and crust shields help prevent burning before the full pie reaches nirvana. You can manually construct a protective barrier with aluminum foil, but if you plan to bake pies with any frequency, I recommend a reusable silicone crust shield. Admittedly, I find the silicone shields a headache to use, particularly once they're hot, since they rely on a tiny, fiddly latch that often comes undone, but they're the best option I've found thus far. The weight of reusable metal shields usually inhibits the full manifestation of those coveted flaky crust layers, so all roads still lead back to silicone despite its foibles. Please contact me ASAP if you invent a better solution.

CUTTERS (ROUND, SHAPE, ALPHABET): Shape cutters are the easiest way to cut uniform pieces of fruits and vegetables, but if you don't have any on hand, you can always manually slice shapes with a knife. (Just clear your calendar and plan to have a dog walker come take your pup out while you are occupied for the next year.) I prefer the sets from Ateco, and they're pretty affordable considering the amount of time they save.

DIGITAL SCALE: They give you better baking accuracy, and you'll have fewer dishes to wash. Need I say more? Okay, I will. Digital scales are also low-cost and eliminate the need for mental math (shudder), which makes them worth their weight in butter.

ELECTRIC MIXER: I have a hand-me-down stand mixer that I recently relegated to the basement to regain counter space real estate, and because it's frankly more than I need. For all the whipped fillings in this book, a simple electric hand mixer will do the trick. Elbow grease and a bit of stamina will also suffice to replace any electronics on this end.

FINE-MESH SIEVE: My 9-inch stainless steel fine-mesh sieve sees heavy rotation. One with a sturdy handle and a hook to rest securely on a mixing bowl is handy in case you too somehow lack a third arm.

FOOD PROCESSOR: Making pie dough by hand results in superior baked flakes, but I've included methods for preparing dough both manually and in a food processor. Leisurely dough preparation can be a luxury, and a food processor serves as a great time (and hand) saver on this front.

KNIVES (PARING AND CHEF'S): Knives are perhaps the most important equipment in any cooking and baking lineup. While you do not need to splurge for high-end brands, nor do you need an extensive number of knives, there is no substitute for a sharp knife you know how to handle well. I love my Tojiro chef's knife for slicing fruit and chopping vegetables, and I use a no-frills $7 Victorinox paring knife for everything else, from cutting precise fruit shapes to trimming excess pie dough to transferring dough pieces for certain designs. The key is ensuring your knives are always nice and sharp!

PASTRY BLENDER: Pastry blenders, along with rodents (see page 119), are my personal nemeses. The ire they provoke in me is tantamount to being noisily wakened from slumber. Unless you want to unleash the beast, it's best to leave me/it well alone (just ask my husband). I find them incredibly aggravating to use, what with butter chunks constantly clumping between the blades and needing to be scraped out. But to each their own. If this is your preferred battle-ax, proceed at your own risk. I mean, our friendship ends here, but you do you, okay?

PASTRY BRUSH: I like to have two sizes in my arsenal—a large silicone brush for egg washing quickly and with abandon and a smaller soft-bristled one for careful and attentive sealing on the more intricate designs. For the latter, I specifically like the ½-inch-wide flat soft-bristle cake brush from Wilton.

PASTRY WHEEL: Sure, a sharp paring knife and a ruler will suffice in a pinch for cutting dough strips, but this little tool is especially handy for executing straight lines with a zip of the hand. Choose one with limited wheel wobble for maximum precision. The Cake Boss version has delivered most reliably for me on this front.

PIE TIN: The USA 9-inch aluminized steel pie tin is far and away my favorite pan to bake with. I get reliably crisp bottoms and slices that slide cleanly out on my command every time. The no-frills Pyrex glass pie dishes are also good options, particularly as they give you a window for checking the doneness of the bottom crust.

PIZZA STONE: One useful method for preventing soggy bottoms is to keep a pizza or

PIE-PELINE: One of the many ironies of this journey is the fact that I don't have a sweet tooth. I could be doomed to eat only savory foods for the rest of my life, and aside from the errant craving for a good churro or yeasted chocolate doughnut, I wouldn't feel bereft. My husband long ago reached pie oversaturation, and since I do not sell the pies, getting rid of them in a sustainable manner posed a problem. Enter the Lokokitchen Pie-peline—an email listserv of all the people I like in Seattle with mouths on which I rely. I send weekly bulletins listing all the items languishing on my dining table, and those who are fast enough to call dibs then swing by my house to collect their spoils. It's a highly effective way to endear people to you and keep food waste at bay. I recommend maintaining a pie-peline in your contacts list should you also require edible assistance (or need friends).

baking stone in your oven. I leave mine in so it gets nice and hot while the oven heats, and I bake the pie (on a rimmed baking sheet, of course) right on top.

ROLLING PIN: I was given a $10 French tapered rolling pin as a wedding gift many years ago. Thank you, kind friend and online registry. It was the only one I owned for many years, so I became accustomed to its weight, shape, and feel for lack of other options. But I still prefer it over other makes and models today. Of all the secrets pies presume to harbor, the type of rolling pin hardly factors, so crust your instincts on this one.

RULER: You may be surprised to discover that I use a ruler less for measuring than I do as a straight line guide, both for cutting dough strips and building patterned fruit lines, but it's handy to have one either way. Stainless steel rulers are ideal, as they can be tossed in the dishwasher and will dry without risk of molding.

SPATULAS (SILICONE AND METAL OFFSET): Flexible silicone spatulas get a lot of mileage in this book between folding fruit fillings, cooking citrus curds, and scraping every last bit of chocolate ganache out of a bowl. Spatulas of the 6-inch metal offset variety are also useful for smoothing the surfaces of tarts and on occasion, transferring fruit and pie dough pieces. You would do well to have both in your baking drawer.

TART PAN: My preferred model is the 9-inch nonstick Wilton tart pan with fluted edges and removable bottom. Unless otherwise specified, I recommend keeping tarts in the pan until the design has been completed. To remove a tart from the pan, gently rest it atop a stable can or cup, allowing the sides to drop away, then move the tart to a secure surface, such as a cutting board, and use a chef's knife to ease the bottom plate off.

PANTRY

I'm supremely fortunate (or actually, my husband is, since he runs most of my errands . . . thanks, Ben!) to have several grocery stores and a farmers' market in the neighborhood. Many of the ingredients called for in this book can be easily found at big-chain or local establishments. A small selection of goods may require a jaunt to the Asian or Latin market or online sourcing.

While I give serious consideration to flavor combinations, color contrast, and texture when embarking on a baking foray, I mainly look to my fruit bowl and refrigerator to inform my direction. Citrus going sideways? Mangoes in mourning? Tomatoes by the ton? I frequently build my tarts or pies around anything getting wrinkly or spilling over in excess. Several recipes throughout the book call for more unusual ingredients, and I list alternative produce when applicable, but be creative with using what you already have or see on sale!

As with the equipment section, the following list is more highlight reel than full feature film.

ALL-PURPOSE FLOUR: Let's be real. I go through so much flour that I buy whatever is the cheapest (looking at you, 20-pound Costco bag). Of course, flour from different brands will behave differently due to varying ratios of protein and starch, but for hobby home-baking purposes, I suspect we won't notice the subtleties. For the sake of conversation, Bob's Red Mill is my splurge brand. (The same approach applies for whole wheat flour.)

BLACK TAHINI: Made from ground, unhulled sesame seeds, black tahini adds deep toasty flavor to desserts. I keep a jar of Kevala in the pantry. Be sure to give tahini a stir to incorporate the separated oil layer before measuring.

BUTTER: What do I really have to say except that I use a *lot* of it? My friends are perpetually shocked when they go to grab a drink from my fridge and find entire shelves packed with blocks of butter. As with all-purpose flour, I favor the cheapest stuff on the shelves, though I do prefer local goods from Darigold when I have the option. But whatever the brand, stick with unsalted.

CHOCOLATE: I personally opt for 70% bittersweet chocolate, but bittersweet,

semisweet, and dark chocolate are all inter-changeable in these recipes.

DRIED FLOWERS: While I use food-grade dried flowers like lavender for flavoring, other blooms, like blue cornflowers (not to be confused with corn flour!) and butterfly pea flowers, are utilized for their coloring. I purchase both online.

EDIBLE FLOWERS: Edible flowers can often be found in the refrigerated herb section of big-chain grocery stores or at your local farmers' market. The blooms used in Floral of the Story (page 272) came from the garden of a friend who was kind enough to shepherd me around to her nontoxic plants. You don't need to shell out for a floral masterpiece, but do take care to forage for unsprayed flowers that are safe for human consumption.

EGGS: The recipes in this book call for large chicken eggs, which usually measure about 2 ounces (56 grams) each.

EXOTIC FRUITS: I lived in South America for several years, and wow, do I miss the luxury of mango and passion fruit trees in inescapable abundance throughout the neighborhood. Now these items come at much higher cost, and sometimes finding them requires dedicated hunting. In the Pacific Northwest, Asian grocery stores are most dependable for produce like papaya, dragon fruit, and lemongrass. As for passion fruit, which is often a rare treasure up here, I buy the frozen puree at the Mexican market to save time and a few bucks.

FRESH FRUIT: Again, opting for what's in season and what's on retail discount is recommended. Firm-ripe fruit is ideal for smooth

slicing and clean cuts for tarts. Softer, much riper fruits are better suited for pie fillings, where a little mush is okay.

FROZEN FRUIT: I prefer not to thaw my frozen fruit before using it in pie fillings, but if you must, drain and either discard or reduce the juices for added flavor (be advised that my recipes do not provide for this step). Frozen fruit is not recommended for tart tops.

FRUIT AND VEGETABLE POWDERS: I prefer to color my pie dough with natural ingredients, because artificial food coloring gives a Play-Doh-like aspect that triggers my gag reflex (sorry for the visual). While I rely on juices to do the bulk of the coloring work, it's not always enough to ensure that the hues hold during baking. Adding a scoop of colored powder is optional but can act as insurance to help maintain the color when heat is applied.

Fruit and vegetable powder tints can vary significantly depending on the brand. Naturally, I encourage you to experiment with your own shades, but I've included my favorite powder brands here for reference. All can be sourced online.

- Micro Ingredients for beet powder
- Bow Hill for blueberry (their blueberry juice is also excellent)
- Wilderness Poets for dragon fruit (pitaya)
- Suncore Foods for butterfly pea flower, blue spirulina, and carrot powders

KOSHER SALT: All recipes in this book were formulated using Crystal Diamond brand kosher salt. Double-check your amounts if you choose to substitute for another brand or salt type, as salt crystal size and thus volume can vary.

MATCHA GREEN TEA POWDER: Matcha can get pricy quickly, but high qualitea goes a long way. Generally, the kind that comes in a metal tin and possesses a more vibrant shade of green will result in brighter dough with less bitterness.

MILK: Unless specified in the recipe, feel free to use the milk of your choice.

MOLASSES: Grandma's brand unsulphured molasses is my go-to. Blackstrap molasses has a different flavor profile and lower moisture content and should not be substituted.

SESAME SEEDS: The biggest difference between black and white sesame seeds is the color; the white seeds are hulled. I love using both for the contrasting hues. While the flavor differences are subtle, black sesame seeds have a slightly deeper, nuttier flavor with a touch of bitterness that works well in desserts. I purchase my sesame seeds toasted from my local Asian market.

SPECULOOS COOKIES (ALSO SPELLED *SPECULAAS*): A Belgian crunchy spiced biscuit reminiscent of gingerbread. The cookies pulverize well to form a fragrant tart crust that tastes and smells like the holidays. I usually reach for the Biscoff brand, which is widely available in grocery stores and online.

SUGAR: Er, see all-purpose flour and butter notes? Again, I'm a hobbyist home baker who hasn't yet won the lottery, so I tend to choose what's most economical. I will often swap brands depending on what's on steepest discount and I haven't experienced adverse consequences from this lack of loyalty. Go with what you like, have in your pantry, or find at your store.

TAPIOCA STARCH (ALSO KNOWN AS TAPIOCA FLOUR): Made from cassava root, tapioca starch is my preferred thickening agent, as it produces a clear gel in contrast to the cloudy fillings that result with cornstarch. Instant tapioca, granulated tapioca, tapioca pearls, and tapioca balls should not be substituted in these recipes.

TART PRIMER

TIPS DON'T LIE

Shakira says "hips don't lie," and while my stiff body and lack of coordination betray me, these pastry pointers never abandon me on the dance floor. Follow along and they won't forsake you, either. Allow them to lead, and you'll be cha-chaing your way to success, fancy fruitwork and all.

MAKING DOUGH: Tart pastry is easier to make than pie dough in that it's much more forgiving. But there is still the risk of over-worked dough, which can result in a tough crust. Keep your butter cold, follow the directions, and don't go overboard with the food processor. You'll be crust fine.

ROLLING DOUGH: I roll out my tart dough directly on the counter, so flouring the surface and my rolling pin before and during the rolling process is crucial. I continuously rotate my dough 45 degrees as I roll to ensure it isn't sticking to the counter, and once I've achieved the desired size I transfer the dough to the tart pan. If you're rolling and the dough isn't moving outward, it's probably stuck to your work surface. Gently pull or scrape it up, flour the surface, and resume. Alternatively, you can roll dough directly on parchment paper or a pastry cloth made of cotton canvas.

Rotating the dough 45 or 90 degrees every few rolls can also help with achieving even circles. Consistently obtaining nicely shaped rolled dough largely comes with repetition and practice, though, so don't stress too much if you're a beginner and find yourself rolling cumulus clouds or other gorgeous blobs instead.

FREEZING TARTS AND DOUGH: Wrapped and rested disks of tart dough can be sealed in a bag or container and frozen for up to four months. Allow the dough to thaw in the refrigerator overnight before rolling.

With the exception of the ice cream tart (Truth or Square, page 75), the tarts in this book are not suitable for freezing. Pastry shells filled with curds and custards don't handle the freezing and thawing process well, and the fresh fruit designs are best, well, fresh. Instant gratification is the name of the game here, so your creations are best consumed within two days of assembly, though day of is ideal.

BAKING TART CRUSTS AND SHELLS: Once you've lined your tart pan tightly with dough and trimmed the edges as directed, save a small ball (about 1 tablespoon) of dough scraps to patch any cracks post-bake. If the baked shell emerges from the oven with outsize cracks beyond minor patching, opt for a thicker filling like the chocolate hazelnut ganache (see page 122) or matcha white chocolate cheesecake (see page 78). Fillings that start as a loose liquid like the egg custard (see page 65) or black tea panna cotta (see page 117) will leak through and cause much tartache.

For all rolled pastry, thoroughly chill the dough in the tart pan in the refrigerator or freezer before baking. This will help prevent shrinkage. Another preventative measure against dough shrinkage is to ensure that the foil lining is pressed tightly into all the inner elbows of the tart and then filling with baking weights.

I always bake tart shells and filled tarts on rimmed baking sheets to catch any errant butter drips while baking, and to provide added stability when transferring the tart in and out of the oven.

REMOVING TARTS FROM THE PAN: Be sure to read each design recipe thoroughly before starting, as some tarts call for the crust to be removed to a plate and others require the shell to remain in the tart pan until the end of the design process.

To remove a tart from the pan, rest it atop a stable can or cup, gently loosening the pan edge with your hands and allowing the sides to drop away. Then move the tart to a flat surface, such as a cutting board, and use a chef's knife to ease the bottom plate off.

CUTTING FINISHED TARTS: Place the tart, removed from the pan, on a cutting board. Use a sharp chef's knife or serrated knife to make small, gentle sawing motions to cut through the fruit or top garnish without destroying the design. Press firmly to cut through the crust. Wipe the knife clean between cuts. Slide the knife under the slice to transfer to a plate.

TART SHELLS

BASIC SHORTBREAD CRUST

I often refer to this as emergency shortbread. Its simplicity makes it the perfect candidate for last-minute dinner parties, surprise houseguests, or sudden midnight cravings, and its humble flavor profile complements any sweet filling. Keep this recipe in your back pocket.

1 cup (142 grams) all-purpose flour

½ cup (57 grams) powdered sugar

½ teaspoon kosher salt

½ cup (1 stick/113 grams) unsalted butter, at room temperature, cut into ½-inch cubes

1. Preheat the oven to 375°F.

2. Combine the flour, powdered sugar, and salt in a medium bowl. Rub the butter into the flour mixture by smushing the cubes with your fingers, working until a homogenous dough forms. The resulting dough should be smooth and supple.

3. Press the dough into a 9-inch tart pan with a removable bottom, using your palm to flatten it into an even layer. Place the tart pan on a baking sheet to catch any butter drips that occur during baking and to provide stability as you transfer the tart shell in and out of the oven.

4. Bake for 17 to 20 minutes, until golden brown.

CHOCOLATE MATCHA SHORTBREAD CRUST

Melodramatic like a proverbial dark and stormy night, this crust is inky in color with a touch of bitterness that pairs especially well with light, fruity whipped creams.

¾ cup (107 grams) all-purpose flour

½ cup (57 grams) powdered sugar

2 tablespoons (11 grams) unsweetened Dutch-process cocoa powder

2 tablespoons (12 grams) matcha green tea powder (see page 16)

½ teaspoon kosher salt

½ cup (1 stick/113 grams) unsalted butter, at room temperature, cut into ½-inch cubes

1. Preheat the oven to 375°F.

2. Sift the flour, powdered sugar, cocoa powder, matcha powder, and salt into a medium bowl and whisk well. Rub the butter cubes into the flour mixture with your fingers, working until a homogenous dough forms. The resulting dough should be smooth and supple.

3. Press the dough into a 9-inch tart pan with a removable bottom, using your palm to flatten it into an even layer. Place the tart pan on a baking sheet to catch any butter drips that occur during baking and to provide stability as you transfer the tart shell in and out of the oven.

4. Bake for 18 to 20 minutes, until the edges are crisp and the crust surface is dry throughout.

FUNFETTI OREO CRUST

With just three ingredients, ten-minute prep time, and a predisposition to play nicely with other crowd favorites like ice cream and peanut butter mousse, this is a crust to celebrate.

24 (282 grams) Oreo sandwich cookies

6 tablespoons (¾ stick/85 grams) unsalted butter, melted

¼ cup (50 grams) rainbow sprinkles

1. Preheat the oven to 350°F.

2. Put the Oreos in a food processor and blitz until the cookies are a uniformly sandy texture. Pour in the melted butter and pulse until the mixture comes together like wet sand. Add the sprinkles and pulse 10 times to distribute (but not obliterate) the sprinkles in the Oreo mixture.

3. Turn the mixture out into a 9-inch tart pan with a removable bottom. Use your fingers to pack the mixture tightly into the pan, going all the way up the sides, then use your palm to flatten the bottom. Make sure the edges and the bottom are compact and of even thickness. Place the tart pan on a baking sheet to catch any butter drips that occur during baking and to provide stability as you transfer the tart shell in and out of the oven.

4. Bake for 8 to 10 minutes, until the crust is no longer shiny with butter. It will continue to crisp up as it cools.

5. Keep the tart shell in the pan, cool completely, and store in the fridge or freezer until ready to fill.

SPECULOOS COOKIE CRUST

Warm, spicy crust seeks peppy, tangy curd for meaningful conversation, foodie adventures, and romantic oven snuggles. Low-maintenance and easy to love.

32 (250 grams) packaged speculoos cookies (see page 17)

6 tablespoons (¾ stick/85 grams) unsalted butter, melted

1. Preheat the oven to 350°F.

2. Put the cookies in a food processor and blitz until the cookies are a uniformly sandy texture. Drizzle in the melted butter and pulse until the mixture comes together like wet sand.

3. Turn the mixture out into a 9-inch tart pan with a removable bottom. Use your fingers to pack the mixture tightly into the pan, going all the way up the sides, then use your palm to flatten the bottom. Make sure the edges and the bottom are compact and of even thickness. Place the tart pan on a baking sheet to catch any butter drips that occur during baking and to provide stability as you transfer the tart shell in and out of the oven.

4. Bake for 8 to 10 minutes, until the crust is no longer shiny with butter. It will continue to crisp up as it cools.

5. Keep the tart shell in the pan, cool completely, and store in the fridge or freezer until ready to fill.

COCONUT PECAN CRUST

Zingy bright curds bring out the best in this nutty crust, but it doesn't balk at creamier fillings like the whipped strawberry cloud (see page 42) or the chocolate hazelnut ganache (see page 122), either.

1 cup (80 grams) unsweetened shredded coconut

1 cup (120 grams) whole shelled pecans

½ cup (78 grams) whole wheat flour

3 tablespoons (37 grams) granulated sugar

½ teaspoon kosher salt

6 tablespoons (¾ stick/85 grams) unsalted butter, melted

1. Preheat the oven to 350°F.

2. Spread the shredded coconut in an even layer on a rimmed baking sheet. Toast the coconut in the oven for 3 minutes, until golden and fragrant. Keep a close eye to ensure it does not burn. Pour the toasted coconut into a food processor.

3. Spread the pecans in an even layer on the baking sheet. Toast the pecans in the oven for 3 to 5 minutes, until deepened in color but not completely dark. Put the toasted nuts with the coconut in the food processor.

4. Add the flour, sugar, and salt to the food processor and blitz until the mixture has a uniformly sandy texture.

5. Pour in the melted butter and pulse until the mixture holds together.

6. Turn the mixture out into a 9-inch tart pan with a removable bottom. Press the mixture firmly into the pan, starting with a ¼-inch-thick edge going all the way up the sides and then using your palm to press the crust evenly into the bottom. Place the tart pan on a baking sheet to catch any butter drips that occur during baking and to provide stability as you transfer the tart shell in and out of the oven.

7. Bake for 23 to 25 minutes, until golden and crisp. If the bottom puffs up during baking, use a flat-bottomed drinking glass to gently press it back down.

8. Keep the tart shell in the pan, cool completely, and place it in a sealed container or wrap it well in plastic until ready to fill.

BASIC TART PASTRY SHELL

This pastry is a blank canvas for painting with wide swathes of sweet or savory creative genius. As with all rolled tart dough in this book, be sure to freeze the dough cold in the tin and line tightly with foil before baking.

1¼ cups (178 grams) all-purpose flour, plus more for rolling out the dough

½ cup (57 grams) powdered sugar

½ teaspoon kosher salt

½ cup (1 stick/113 grams) cold unsalted butter, cut into ½-inch cubes

1 large egg

1. Put the flour, powdered sugar, and salt in a food processor and pulse 5 times to incorporate. Sprinkle in the butter cubes and pulse 15 times to break up the butter. Add the egg and pulse quickly 25 times, until the dough begins to come together.

2. Turn the mixture out onto your work surface and gently press it into a flattened disk with your hands. Resist the urge to knead. Wrap the dough tightly in plastic and let it rest in the refrigerator for at least 30 minutes, or overnight.

3. Roll the dough into an 11-inch circle on a lightly floured surface. Carefully roll the dough onto your rolling pin and gently unfurl it over a 9-inch tart pan with a removable bottom. Gently ease the dough into the inner elbows of the pan. Take care not to stretch the dough to fit the pan, as this contributes to dough shrinkage when baking.

4. Trim the edges of the dough using kitchen shears, leaving a ½-inch overhang. Fold the dough overhang back into the pan and press to adhere the dough, nestling it securely into the fluted border. Run a paring knife parallel to your work surface along the top edge of the tart pan to trim any excess dough. Freeze for at least 30 minutes.

5. Preheat the oven to 350°F.

6. Line the frozen tart shell tightly with foil, ensuring the corner crevices are snug. Fill with baking weights all the way to the top. Place the tart pan on a baking sheet.

7. *To partially bake the crust*, bake the shell with the weights for 22 to 25 minutes, until the foil no longer sticks to the dough. Carefully remove the foil and weights and bake for 5 to 10 minutes more. The tart shell should look pale but not raw.

To fully bake the crust, bake the shell with the weights for 22 to 25 minutes, remove the foil and weights, and bake for 15 to 17 minutes, until the shell is dry. A fully baked tart shell can be made 1 to 2 days in advance.

CHOCOLATE TART PASTRY SHELL

Mildly chocolaty, this pastry shell is versatile when it comes to mixing and matching with a range of sweet fillings and fruit toppings. It's an adaptable foundation for building your own creation!

1 cup (142 grams) all-purpose flour, plus more for rolling out the dough

½ cup (57 grams) powdered sugar

3 tablespoons (15 grams) unsweetened Dutch-process cocoa powder

½ teaspoon kosher salt

½ cup (1 stick/113 grams) cold unsalted butter, cut into ½-inch cubes

1 large egg

1. Put the flour, powdered sugar, cocoa powder, and salt in a food processor and pulse 5 times to incorporate. Sprinkle in the butter cubes and pulse quickly 15 times to break up the butter. Add the egg and pulse quickly 25 times. The texture of the dough should resemble a big bowl of Dippin' Dots ice cream.

2. Turn the mixture out onto your work surface and gently press the dough into a flattened disk with your hands. Wrap it tightly in plastic and let it rest in the refrigerator for at least 30 minutes, or overnight.

3. Roll the dough into an 11-inch circle on a lightly floured surface. Carefully roll the dough onto your rolling pin and gently unfurl it over a 9-inch tart pan with a removable bottom. Gently ease the dough into the inner elbows of the pan. Take care not to stretch the dough to fit the pan, as this contributes to dough shrinkage when baking.

4. Trim the edges of the dough using kitchen shears, leaving a ½-inch overhang. Fold the dough overhang back into the pan and press to adhere the dough, nestling it securely into the fluted border. Run a paring knife parallel to your work surface along the top edge of the tart pan to trim any excess dough. Freeze for at least 30 minutes.

5. Preheat the oven to 350°F.

6. Line the frozen tart shell tightly with foil, ensuring the corner crevices are snug. Fill with baking weights all the way to the top. Place the tart pan on a baking sheet to catch any butter drips that occur during baking and to provide stability as you transfer the tart shell in and out of the oven.

7. *To partially bake the crust*, bake the shell with weights for 22 to 25 minutes, until the foil no longer sticks to the dough. Carefully remove the foil and weights and bake for 5 to 10 minutes more. The tart shell should be neither raw nor fully crisp at this point.

To fully bake the crust, bake the shell with the weights for 22 to 25 minutes, remove the weights, and bake for 15 to 17 minutes, until the shell is dry. A fully baked tart shell can be made 1 to 2 days in advance. Be sure to wrap well once cooled to maintain freshness.

TART SHELLS

MATCHA GREEN TEA TART PASTRY SHELL

A matcha pastry shell is a vehicle for injecting maximum color into a design, but she's not just beauty, she's brains, too. The earthy green tea notes are especially wonderful for balancing sweeter fillings.

1 cup (142 grams) all-purpose flour, plus more for rolling out the dough

½ cup (57 grams) powdered sugar

3 tablespoons (18 grams) matcha green tea powder (see page 16)

½ teaspoon kosher salt

½ cup (1 stick/113 grams) cold butter, cut into ½-inch cubes

1 large egg

1 tablespoon milk

1. Put the flour, powdered sugar, matcha powder, and salt in a food processor and pulse 5 times to incorporate. Sprinkle the butter cubes over the dry mixture and pulse 15 times to break up the butter. Add the egg and milk and pulse quickly 25 times, until the dough begins to come together.

2. Turn the mixture out onto your work surface and gently press it into a flattened disk with your hands. Wrap it tightly in plastic and let it rest in the refrigerator for at least 30 minutes, or overnight.

3. Roll the dough into an 11-inch circle on a lightly floured surface. Carefully roll the dough onto your rolling pin and gently unfurl it over a 9-inch tart pan with a removable bottom. Ease the dough into the inner elbows of the pan. Take care not to stretch the dough to fit the pan, as this contributes to dough shrinkage when baking.

4. Trim the edges of the dough using kitchen shears, leaving a ½-inch overhang. Fold the dough overhang back into the pan and press to adhere the dough, nestling it securely into the fluted border. Run a paring knife parallel to your work surface along the top edge of the tart pan to trim any excess dough. Freeze for at least 30 minutes.

5. Preheat the oven to 350°F.

6. Line the frozen tart shell tightly with foil, ensuring the corner crevices are snug. Fill with baking weights all the way to the top. Place the tart pan on a baking sheet to catch any butter drips that occur during baking and to provide stability as you transfer the tart shell in and out of the oven.

7. For baking instructions, refer to step 8 of the Basic Tart Pastry Shell (page 31).

EVERYTHING (BUT THE) BAGEL TART PASTRY SHELL

No one will fault you for making this pastry for the aroma alone. Inhale, exhale, and if you're not completely immobilized from the fragrance, proceed by completing the tart with any of the savory fillings in this book.

1 cup (142 grams) all-purpose flour, plus more for rolling out the dough

1 tablespoon (9 grams) black sesame seeds (see page 17)

1 tablespoon (9 grams) white sesame seeds

1 tablespoon (9 grams) poppy seeds

1 tablespoon (10 grams) dried minced garlic

1 tablespoon (10 grams) dried minced onion

1 teaspoon kosher salt

½ cup (1 stick/113 grams) cold unsalted butter, cut into ½-inch cubes

1 large egg

2 tablespoons milk

1. Put the flour, black and white sesame seeds, poppy seeds, garlic, onion, and salt in a food processor and pulse 5 times to incorporate. Sprinkle the butter cubes over the dry mixture and pulse 15 times to break up the butter. Add the egg and milk and pulse quickly 25 times, until the dough begins to come together.

2. Turn the mixture out onto your work surface and gently press it into a flattened disk with your hands. Wrap it tightly in plastic and let it rest in the refrigerator for at least 30 minutes, or overnight.

3. Roll the dough into an 11-inch circle on a lightly floured surface. Carefully roll the dough onto your rolling pin and gently unfurl it over a 9-inch tart pan with a removable bottom. Gently ease the dough into the inner elbows of the pan. Take care not to stretch the dough to fit the pan, as this contributes to dough shrinkage when baking.

4. Trim the edges of the dough using kitchen shears, leaving a ½-inch overhang. Fold the dough overhang back into the pan and press to adhere the dough, nestling it securely into the fluted border. Run a paring knife parallel to your work surface along the top edge of the tart pan to trim any excess dough. Freeze for at least 30 minutes.

5. Preheat the oven to 350°F.

6. Line the frozen tart shell tightly with foil, ensuring the corner crevices are snug. Fill with baking weights all the way to the top. Place the tart pan on a baking sheet to catch any butter drips that occur during baking and to provide stability as you transfer the tart shell in and out of the oven.

7. *To partially bake the crust*, bake the shell with the weights for 22 to 25 minutes, until the foil no longer sticks to the dough. Carefully remove the foil and weights and bake for 5 to 10 minutes more. The tart shell should look pale but not raw.

To fully bake the crust, bake the shell with the weights for 22 to 25 minutes, remove the weights, and bake for 15 to 17 minutes, until the shell is dry. A fully baked tart shell can be made 1 to 2 days in advance. Be sure to wrap well once cooled to maintain freshness.

HERBED TART PASTRY SHELL

Use this herbed pastry like the Everything (but the) Bagel pastry—smother it in all manner of cheese and veg. Breakfast, lunch, and dinner sorted.

1¼ cups (178 grams) all-purpose flour, plus more for rolling out the dough

5 small fresh basil leaves, finely chopped

2 teaspoons finely chopped fresh chives

1 teaspoon fresh thyme leaves

1 teaspoon kosher salt

½ cup (1 stick/113 grams) cold unsalted butter, cut into ½-inch cubes

1 large egg

2 tablespoons milk

1. Put the flour, basil, chives, thyme, and salt in a food processor and pulse 5 times to incorporate. Sprinkle the butter cubes over the dry mixture and pulse 15 times to break up the butter. Add the egg and milk and pulse quickly 25 times, until the dough begins to come together.

2. Turn the mixture out onto your work surface and gently press it into a flattened disk with your hands. Wrap it tightly in plastic and let it rest in the refrigerator for at least 30 minutes, or overnight.

3. Roll the dough into an 11-inch circle on a lightly floured surface. Carefully roll the dough onto your rolling pin and gently unfurl it over a 9-inch tart pan with a removable bottom. Gently ease the dough into the inner elbows of the pan. Take care not to stretch the dough to fit the pan, as this contributes to dough shrinkage when baking.

4. Trim the edges of the dough using kitchen shears, leaving a ½-inch overhang. Fold the dough overhang back into the pan and press to adhere the dough, nestling it securely into the fluted border. Run a paring knife parallel to your work surface along the top edge of the tart pan to trim any excess dough. Freeze for at least 30 minutes.

5. Preheat the oven to 350°F.

6. Line the frozen tart shell tightly with foil, ensuring the corner crevices are snug. Fill with baking weights all the way to the top. Place the tart pan on a baking sheet to catch any butter drips that occur during baking and to provide stability as you transfer the tart shell in and out of the oven.

7. *To partially bake the crust*, bake the shell with weights for 22 to 25 minutes, until the foil no longer sticks to the dough. Carefully remove the foil and weights and bake for 5 to 10 minutes more. The tart shell should look pale but not raw.

To fully bake the crust, bake the shell with weights for 22 to 25 minutes, remove the weights, and bake for 15 to 17 minutes, until the shell is dry. A fully baked tart shell can be made 1 to 2 days in advance. Be sure to wrap well once cooled to maintain freshness.

TART ART

SWIRLED PEACE

I have a degree in international relations, and while most of my days spent as a pie lady feel a far cry from my original career path, this tart indicates that overlap may exist after all. The crisp chocolate matcha shortbread paired with a fluffy strawberry cloud and a crown of perfumed apricots may very well be the path to world peace. Should you ever find yourself in a sticky situation, consider this a sanctioned diplomatic stratagem.

1 baked Chocolate Matcha Shortbread Crust (page 27)

WHIPPED STRAWBERRY CLOUD

½ cup (118 milliliters) heavy cream

1 cup (20 grams) freeze-dried strawberries

1 cup (8 ounces/226 grams) mascarpone cheese

½ cup (57 grams) powdered sugar

⅓ cup (79 milliliters) milk

1. In a medium bowl, whip the heavy cream to soft peaks with an electric mixer. Set aside.

2. Pulverize the strawberries into a powder with a spice grinder or by placing them in a zip-top bag and pounding them to smithereens with a rolling pin.

3. Put the mascarpone in a large bowl and sift in the strawberry powder and powdered sugar. Beat with an electric mixer until well incorporated. The mixture will be very thick. Add the milk and beat until smooth and fluffy, about 2 minutes.

4. Gently fold in the whipped cream with a spatula until just combined.

5. Remove the cooled crust from the tart pan and place it securely on a plate. Dollop the whipped strawberry cream in the center and spread it evenly over the surface of the crust with an offset spatula, leaving a ¼-inch edge of exposed crust.

APRICOT SWIRL DESIGN PROCESS

4 or 5 firm-ripe apricots

Chef's knife

1. Halve and pit the apricots. Cut each apricot half into 8 wedges. If any of your apricot slices have a reddish color variation in the skin and you want to incorporate an ombré effect into your design, organize the slices by color on a plate.

2. Beginning from the outer edge of the tart, wedge one apricot slice skin-side up into the cream. Insert another apricot slice to the inside of the first one, staggering its placement. If you are constructing an ombré, start with a few of your

darkest-colored slices and gradually transition to lighter-colored slices. Do not use all the red slices in this ring.

3. Continue following the curved edge of the tart. Once you've completed a full rotation, without breaking the line, continue arranging apricots tightly inside the first ring in the same staggered overlap. If you're ombré-ing, incorporate a handful more of the red slices, gradually transitioning to lighter shades.

4. Keep spiraling inward on the surface of the tart. If the remaining space in the center is inhibiting, cut an apricot slice to size.

5. Keep in the refrigerator until ready to serve. This tart is best consumed the day it is made. For a clean slice, use a sharp chef's knife or serrated knife to make small, gentle sawing motions to cut through the fruit without destroying the design. Press firmly to cut through the crust. Wipe the knife clean between cuts. Slide the knife under the slice to transfer to a plate.

SUGGESTED SUBSTITUTIONS

Crust alternatives: Basic Shortbread Crust (page 26), Funfetti Oreo Crust (page 28)

Topping alternatives: Plums, peaches, cherries, berries

NOTE

If you have any leftover apricot slices, freeze them in a single layer on a baking sheet and then seal in a container once frozen. The frozen apricot slices can be tossed into a pie like Lattice Quo (page 220).

While apartment hunting in Paraguay, I stumbled onto an inviting corner unit. It looked promising from the outside, but it was immediately clear upon entry that it was too spacious for me alone. Still, I wanted the complete tour. I wandered through the palatial master bedroom and slid open the screen door to reveal a balcony overlooking a flower garden. The charm was undeniable, and though it was out of my budget, I was already mentally unpacking my belongings.

I opened a wooden armoire and a blur of black shot out and slammed on the ground, shaking me out of my reverie. It was a bat. A BAT. It attempted several feeble flops around the tile floor and then promptly died. I beat a hasty retreat, and will never think about that dwelling without a shudder.

The place I eventually chose was a quaint abode with a little patio just big enough for a single hammock and a kitchen marked by the half gallon of lime juice I spent hours extracting by hand and then dropped. The acidity stripped the floor polish in an extravagant splash pattern that resembled—what else—a giant bat, and persisted for the duration of my two-year residence.

Lime juice will forever be linked to these memories for me. Fortunately, there aren't any winged creatures involved here unless you consider *dragon* fruit to be in the same cursed category. But the vivid magenta powder produces such an alluring hue that sparkles against the fresh fruit, I promise you won't even bat an eye.

1 baked Coconut Pecan Crust (page 30)

DRAGON FRUIT LIME CURD

½ cup (99 grams) granulated sugar

3 tablespoons (18 grams) dragon fruit (pitaya) powder (see page 16)

½ teaspoon kosher salt

½ cup (119 milliliters) fresh lime juice, from about 5 limes

2 large eggs plus 2 egg yolks

4 tablespoons (½ stick/57 grams) unsalted butter, cut into ½-inch cubes

1. Preheat the oven to 350°F.

2. Combine the sugar, dragon fruit powder, and salt in a 2-quart saucepan and whisk well, eliminating any lumps. Add the lime juice, eggs, and egg yolks and cook over medium heat, whisking continuously, until the mixture is warmed through. Add the butter gradually and stir with a spatula until all the cubes have melted. Continue cooking until the mixture has thickened and coats the spatula, 5 to 8 minutes, stirring frequently and scraping the corners of the saucepan.

3. Remove from the heat and strain the curd through a fine-mesh sieve.

4. Keep the baked tart shell in the tart pan and place it on a baking sheet. Pour the curd into the tart shell and smooth the surface.

5. Bake the tart for 5 minutes, just to set the filling.

6. Cool completely before decorating.

PARALLELOGRAM TILE DESIGN PROCESS

1 ripe white-fleshed dragon fruit (pitaya)

1½-inch rhombus cutter (see the photo on page 10)

Paring knife

Ruler

1. Trim and peel the dragon fruit and cut it into ¼-inch slices. Using the rhombus cutter, punch out at least 28 shapes from the dragon fruit slices. Try to maximize the number of shapes cut from each slice of fruit to minimize scraps, which, in any case, make a great bonus snack while you are working, or you can freeze them for future smoothies.

2. Cut each rhombus in half to create two identical parallelograms.

3. Lay a ruler vertically down the center of the tart, resting it on the edges of the pan. Following the ruler edge, lightly trace a line down the tart with a toothpick or the tip of your knife. Remove the ruler.

4. Starting at the top of the tart, place a dragon fruit parallelogram with its short edge on the marked line. Take another parallelogram, flipped to be the mirror image of the first parallelogram, and place it on the other side of the line. The top corner of the second parallelogram should touch the bottom corner of the first parallelogram.

5. Continue laying parallelograms down the line, alternating sides. Keep placing dragon fruit pieces in this fashion until the entire surface of the tart has been covered.

6. Keep in the refrigerator until ready to serve. This tart is best consumed within 2 days. For a clean slice, use a sharp chef's knife or serrated knife to make small, gentle sawing motions to cut through the fruit without destroying the design. Press firmly to cut through the crust. Wipe the knife clean between cuts. Slide the knife under the slice to transfer to a plate.

SUGGESTED SUBSTITUTIONS

Crust alternatives: Speculoos Cookie Crust (page 29), Basic Tart Pastry Shell (page 31), Matcha Green Tea Tart Pastry Shell (page 35)

Topping alternatives: Mango, papaya, pineapple, kiwi

NOTES

A small offset spatula and culinary tweezers can be useful for transferring dragon fruit shapes and nudging fruit into place, respectively. Otherwise, a paring knife is perfectly adequate for fulfilling both these roles.

Opportunities to utilize leftover dragon fruit: Happy as a Gram (page 51), Hex and Balances (page 81), Livin' on a Pair (page 86).

À LA CODE

I taught myself how to write backward just for funsies in middle school (nerd alert!), and in that antiquated pre–text messaging era, would write all my friends notes in backward script. They would have to flip the page into the light or hold it up to a mirror to read.

I daresay this code—a simple combination of chocolate pastry, raspberry lemon curd, and melon messaging—is decidedly easier to craft and decipher. Take your best crack at it!

1 fully baked Chocolate Tart Pastry Shell (page 32)

PINK LEMONADE CURD

1 cup (4 ounces/125 grams) fresh red raspberries

½ cup (118 milliliters) fresh lemon juice, from about 4 lemons

Zest of 1 lemon

½ cup (99 grams) granulated sugar

½ teaspoon kosher salt

2 large eggs plus 2 egg yolks

4 tablespoons (½ stick/57 grams) unsalted butter, cut into ½-inch cubes

1. Preheat the oven to 350°F.

2. Press the raspberries through a fine-mesh sieve into a 2-quart saucepan using a silicone spatula, scraping to extract as much puree as possible. Discard the remaining seeds.

3. Add the lemon juice, lemon zest, sugar, salt, eggs, and egg yolks to the saucepan with the raspberry puree and whisk to combine. Cook over medium heat, whisking continuously, until the mixture is warmed through. Add the butter gradually and stir until all the cubes have melted. Continue cooking until the mixture is thick enough to coat a spatula, 5 to 8 minutes, stirring frequently and scraping the corners of the saucepan.

4. Remove from the heat and strain the curd through a fine-mesh sieve.

5. Keep the baked tart shell in the tart pan and place on a baking sheet. Pour the curd into the tart shell and smooth the surface.

6. Bake the tart for 5 minutes, just to set the filling.

7. Cool completely before decorating.

PIEOMETRY

ALIEN CODE DESIGN PROCESS

1 small cantaloupe

1 small honeydew melon

1-inch square cutter

1-inch circle cutter

1 × ½-inch rectangle cutter

Chef's knife

Paring knife

Ruler

1. Slice the cantaloupe in half and scoop out the seeds. Keep half on your work space, and reserve the other half for another tart or to wrap with prosciutto for dinner! Do the same for the honeydew melon.

2. Place each melon half cut-side down and slice into ¼-inch slices.

3. Using 1-inch shape cutters, punch out an assortment of squares, rectangles, and circles from the melon slices, avoiding the skin. Cut all the shapes in half—the circles into half moons, the squares into rectangles, and the rectangles into right triangles.

4. Lay a ruler horizontally across the tart, one inch from the top, resting the ruler on the edges of the pan. Starting from the left edge of the tart, construct a 1-inch row of alien code, varying the fruits and shapes in a freestyle arrangement as you go along. For the uninitiated, my code here roughly translates to "One melon light-years from the pun." Jury's out if extraterrestrials also find my jokes alien.

5. When the first row has been completed, move the ruler down 1½ inches to allow a ½-inch gap between rows. Continue laying down code, alternating between shapes and their directional placement, until the entire surface of the tart has been covered.

6. Keep in the refrigerator until ready to serve. This tart is best consumed within 2 days.

SUGGESTED SUBSTITUTIONS

Crust alternatives: Speculoos Cookie Crust (page 29), Coconut Pecan Crust (page 30), Basic Tart Pastry Shell (page 31)

Topping alternatives: Mango, papaya, pineapple, kiwi, dragon fruit

HAPPY AS A GRAM

I've never been very mathematically inclined, as my brain has always been more adept at arranging words than numbers. The amount of nights I've cried over frustrating problem sets I couldn't solve over my lifetime is incalculable. That I've been able to contribute anything to the discipline of pieometry seems incongruent with my history, but as we know, life rarely moves in a straight line, and the thrill of this unforeseen angle has been acute.

Inspired by the tangram, a Chinese dissection puzzle made up of geometric shapes arranged in varying combinations to form other shapes, this design is one that has come to define the Lokokitchen aesthetic. While the concept is derived through coplanar placement of polygons and assorted angles, don't get bogged down by the formula. Ultimately, the sum of its parts is simply a tart, and variables will translate, too.

1 baked Speculoos Cookie Crust (page 29)

CRANBERRY CURD

15 ounces (425 grams) cranberries, fresh or frozen

3 tablespoons fresh lemon juice

¾ cup (149 grams) granulated sugar

½ teaspoon kosher salt

3 large eggs plus 2 egg yolks

6 tablespoons (85 grams) butter, at room temperature, cut into ½-inch cubes

1. Preheat the oven to 350°F.

2. Combine the cranberries and 2 tablespoons water in a 2-quart saucepan. Stir over medium heat until the cranberries burst and start to break down, about 5 minutes. Remove from the heat and press the cranberries through a fine-mesh sieve with a silicone spatula, extracting as much puree as possible. Discard the remaining pulp and return the puree to the saucepan.

3. Add the lemon juice, sugar, salt, eggs, and egg yolks to the cranberry puree and whisk to combine. Cook over medium heat, whisking continuously, until the mixture is warmed through. Add the butter gradually and stir until all the cubes have melted. Continue cooking until the mixture is thickened enough to coat a spatula, 5 to 8 minutes, stirring frequently and scraping the corners of the saucepan.

4. Remove from the heat and strain the curd through a fine-mesh sieve.

5. Keep the baked tart shell in the tart pan and place on a baking sheet. Pour the curd into the tart shell, smoothing the surface. Bake the tart for 5 minutes, just to set the filling.

6. Cool completely before decorating.

TANGRAM DESIGN PROCESS

1 firm mango

1 white-fleshed dragon fruit (pitaya)

2 or 3 firm kiwis

Chef's knife

1. Peel and cut the fruit into ¼-inch slices. Arrange the fruit slices on a large plate organized by type.

2. Cut any type of triangle—equilateral, scalene, obtuse, acute, isosceles, right—from a piece of mango, slicing as close to the edge as possible to maximize the yield of each fruit slice. Pause here if you feel the need to Google image search

recipe continues

some triangles. Otherwise, throw math to the wind and cut any sort of shape with three sides. Place it along a tart edge.

3. Cut another shape from a kiwi slice and place it next to the mango, leaving some space between the fruit, not unlike tile grout lines. Generally, polygons like triangles, parallelograms, and trapezoids work well for this design. I avoid shapes with more than four sides mainly to save time, but if manually sliced hexagons or even hendecagons (back to Google . . .) are your thing, by all means, go wild! This is your tart, your life.

4. Cut another shape, perhaps a rhombus, from a slice of dragon fruit, and fit it next to the kiwi. Continue cutting shapes, alternating among fruits, and puzzling the pieces together on the tart. Build out from your starting point and slowly fill the whole surface, gradually working your way to the other edge.

5. Keep in the refrigerator until ready to serve. This tart is best consumed within 2 days.

SUGGESTED SUBSTITUTIONS

Crust alternatives: Coconut Pecan Crust (page 30), Basic Tart Pastry Shell (page 31)

Topping alternatives: Papaya, pineapple, persimmon

NOTE

For design alternatives, you can opt to use a single variety of fruit for a monochromatic aesthetic, and you can also arrange your tangrams to cover only a crescent-shaped area of the surface rather than the full slate.

OF A SHINGLE MIND

One humid summer when I lived in Boston, my weekly CSA (community-supported agriculture) box inundated me with pounds and pounds of beets. My feelings toward the vegetable were tepid to begin with and quickly burgeoned into searing animosity after months of unrelenting surplus. It fueled many a culinary nightmare for years after, and to this day, the earthy flavor of beets continues to haunt me. Fortunately, the cheese and roasted garlic in this tart offset the beet's worst qualities and mellow everything out, including the root (pun always intended) of my anxiety. So if you too feel wary about delving into the murky world of root veg, this approach for easing into it is unbeetable.

1 partially baked Herbed Tart Pastry Shell (page 38)

HONEY RICOTTA BEET FILLING

1 large red beet (about 1 pound/454 grams)

1 large Chioggia beet (about 1 pound/454 grams)

3 large garlic cloves, unpeeled

1 cup (250 grams) ricotta

1 large egg

3 tablespoons (63 grams) honey

1 teaspoon balsamic vinegar

½ teaspoon kosher salt, or more as desired

½ teaspoon freshly ground black pepper, or more as desired

1. Preheat the oven to 400°F.

2. Scrub the beets and pat dry. Trim the ends and wrap each beet individually in foil. Wrap the garlic cloves in foil. Roast the beets and garlic on a rimmed baking sheet until fork-tender, 35 to 50 minutes.

3. Lower the oven temperature to 350°F.

4. When the beets are cool enough to handle, rub off and discard the skins and cut the beets into ⅛-inch slices. Using a 1-inch oval cutter, punch out at least 50 shapes—25 red and 25 striped. Measure 3 ounces of beets (about ½ cup) from the scraps and place them in a food processor.

5. Squeeze the roasted garlic into the food processor with the beet scraps, discarding the peels. Add the ricotta, egg, 2 tablespoons of the honey, the vinegar, salt, and pepper. Pulse to blend until smooth. Season to taste with additional salt and pepper as desired.

6. Place the partially baked shell in its tart pan on a rimmed baking sheet. Pour the ricotta filling into the shell and smooth the surface.

BEET SHINGLE DESIGN PROCESS

1-inch oval cutter (used in step 4 above)

1. Beginning at the top of the tart, lay a horizontal row of overlapping red beet ovals. Do not let the beet ovals touch the tart crust, as the beet juice may cause the shell to become soggy during baking.

2. Next, lay a row of overlapping Chioggia beet ovals. This row should slightly overlap with the row of red beets. Continue laying rows of overlapping beets down the tart, alternating colors with each row, until the surface has been covered.

3. Bake the tart for 30 to 35 minutes. Drizzle the remaining 1 tablespoon honey over the surface of the tart while still hot. The tart can be served hot, at room temperature, or chilled. This tart is best consumed within 2 days.

SUGGESTED SUBSTITUTIONS

Crust alternative: Everything (but the) Bagel Tart Pastry Shell (page 36)

Topping alternative: A golden beet can be substituted for the Chioggia beet, but prioritize using red beet scraps when measuring for the filling in order to achieve the vibrant pink color.

SWIM WITH THE SPARKS

As I'm a shy introvert, moving to a new city and building community from scratch is akin to swimming with sharks. I've muddled my way through many a happy hour and, in spite of my particular cocktail of awkwardness and quirk, I've collected a congenial cohort of chums! My preferred drinks are ones that are smoky, spicy, sour, and a tinge sweet: elements I've infused into this tart as an ode to the lovely people that round out my crew. Cheers!

Please note that this recipe requires an overnight step before assembly!

1 fully baked Basic Tart Pastry Shell (page 31)

BLOOD ORANGE CHIPOTLE CURD

2 cups (473 milliliters) fresh blood orange juice, from about 15 oranges, plus the zest of 1 blood orange

1 ounce (28 grams) whole dried chipotle peppers (3 to 6 peppers)

½ cup (99 grams) granulated sugar

½ teaspoon kosher salt

3 large eggs plus 3 egg yolks

6 tablespoons (¾ stick/85 grams) unsalted butter, cut into ½-inch cubes

½ tablespoon mezcal (optional)

PREPARE A DAY AHEAD

1. Combine the blood orange juice (reserve the zest in the refrigerator for the next day) and chipotle peppers in a small saucepan over medium-high heat. Bring the juice to a boil, turn down the heat to medium-low, and cook until reduced to ¾ cup (177 milliliters) liquid, 25 to 35 minutes. Cool, cover, and steep the peppers in the orange juice overnight in the refrigerator.

DAY OF

2. Preheat the oven to 350°F.

3. Strain the reduced juice into a small saucepan. Rinse and dry the peppers, place them in a sealed container, and reserve in the refrigerator for a future use.

4. Add the sugar, salt, orange zest, eggs, and egg yolks to the saucepan and whisk to combine well. Cook over medium heat, whisking continuously, until the mixture has warmed through. Add the butter gradually and stir until all the cubes have melted. Continue cooking until the mixture is thick enough to coat a spatula, 5 to 8 minutes, stirring frequently and scraping the corners of the saucepan. Remove from the heat. If using, whisk in the mezcal.

5. Strain the curd through a fine-mesh sieve.

6. Keep the baked tart shell in the tart pan and place on a baking sheet. Pour the curd into the tart shell and smooth the surface.

7. Bake the tart for 5 minutes, just to set the filling.

8. Cool completely before decorating.

1 firm mango

1 tablespoon chile lime salt, such as Tajín (optional)

Chef's knife

Paring knife

1. Peel the mango and cut it into ¼-inch slices. Stand over the sink and gnaw the remaining flesh off the seed with abandon, then wash your face and proceed with the recipe.

2. Cut an assortment of skinny triangles from the mango slices and arrange them in a single layer on a plate. If using, sprinkle a handful of pieces with the chile lime salt.

3. Using a toothpick or the point of your knife, lightly mark the center of the tart for reference. Place approximately 7 mango sparks, inserting chile-dusted sparks as desired, radiating around the center point. The apexes should be touching in the center and the triangles otherwise spaced evenly.

4. Insert mango sparks into the gaps between the first ring of triangles. The spark apexes should be offset from the center point, and the triangles should not touch. Randomly add chile-dusted sparks between the plain sparks.

5. Continue working your way outward on the tart surface by inserting mango into the spaces in between. As you reach the outermost edge of the tart, trim the mango sparks to fit.

6. Keep the tart in the refrigerator until ready to serve. If not serving the same day, cover lightly with plastic to prevent the mango sparks from drying out. This tart is best consumed within 2 days.

SUGGESTED SUBSTITUTIONS

Crust alternatives: Coconut Pecan Crust (page 30), Chocolate Tart Pastry Shell (page 32)

Filling alternatives: Cara Cara oranges, grapefruit (increase the sugar to 1 cup/198 grams)

Topping alternatives: Papaya, pineapple, kiwi

When Ben and I traveled to Peru, we arrived in Cusco early to acclimate to the high elevation before embarking on our Machu Picchu trek. We walked very slowly around town, combatting our altitude sickness by drinking all the tea and eating every alfajor in sight. One café we ducked into offered a steaming beverage with fresh slices of lemon and grapefruit muddled with coca leaves and stalks of lemongrass. Years later, I haven't stopped thinking about that zesty combination.

While I've traded coca leaves for pineapple here (the stimulant is illegal in the United States, after all), the tangy curd in this tart still retains all the best of the original brew's refreshing, piquant qualities and is one that is sure to stick with you, too.

Please note that this recipe requires an overnight step before assembly!

1 fully baked Basic Tart Pastry Shell (page 31)

GRAPEFRUIT LEMONGRASS CURD

3 stalks (8 ounces/227 grams) fresh lemongrass

2 cups (474 milliliters) fresh grapefruit juice, from about 3 large grapefruits

½ cup (118 milliliters) fresh lime juice, from about 5 limes

½ cup (99 grams) granulated sugar

½ teaspoon kosher salt

2 large eggs plus 3 egg yolks

6 tablespoons (85 grams) unsalted butter, cut into ½-inch cubes

PREPARE A DAY AHEAD

1. Rinse the lemongrass stalks and peel away the first few tough layers. Roughly chop the remaining stalks into 1-inch pieces and use a mortar and pestle or the side of your chef's knife to bruise the lemongrass.

2. Combine the crushed lemongrass, grapefruit juice, and lime juice in a small saucepan over medium-high heat. Bring the juice to a boil, turn the heat to medium-low, and cook to reduce to 1 cup (237 milliliters) of liquid, about 25 minutes. Cool, cover, and steep the lemongrass in the grapefruit juice overnight in the refrigerator.

DAY OF

3. Preheat the oven to 350°F.

4. Strain the reduced liquid and discard the lemongrass. Combine the infused grapefruit juice, sugar, salt, eggs, and egg yolks in a 2-quart saucepan and whisk well. Cook over medium heat, stirring continuously, until the mixture is warmed through. Add the butter gradually and stir until all the cubes have melted. Continue cooking until the mixture is thick enough to coat a spatula, 5 to 8 minutes, stirring frequently and scraping the corners of the saucepan. Remove from the heat and strain the curd through a fine-mesh sieve.

recipe continues

5. Keep the baked tart shell in the tart pan and place it on a baking sheet. Pour the curd into the tart shell and smooth the surface.

6. Bake the tart for 5 to 10 minutes to just set the filling. The edges should be solid while the center retains the slightest of jiggles.

7. Cool completely before decorating.

PINEAPPLE MATCHSTICK DESIGN PROCESS

1 pineapple

Chef's knife

1. Trim and peel the pineapple. Cut the fruit in half lengthwise, reserving one half for another use. Halve the pineapple lengthwise again and slice out the core. Cut the wedges into ¼-inch slices.

2. Cut the slices into matchsticks measuring approximately 1 × ¼ inch. Slight variations in size can bring a fun textural element to this design, though, so don't stress about perfection.

3. Lay a ruler across the surface of the tart 1½ inches from the top, resting it on the edges of the tart pan. Place a horizontal row of vertical matchsticks, separated by ⅛ inch, using the tip of a paring knife to nudge the fruit pieces into place.

4. When the first row has been completed, slide the ruler down 1½ inches to create a straight line reference for row 2. Continue the same process of placing vertical matchsticks. Repeat row by row until the entire surface of the tart has been covered, trimming pineapple pieces to fit as needed.

5. Keep in the refrigerator until ready to serve. This tart is best consumed within 2 days.

SUGGESTED SUBSTITUTIONS

Crust alternative: Coconut Pecan Crust (page 30)

Topping alternatives: Mango, papaya, kiwi, dragon fruit. If you have an assortment of tropical fruit scraps from other designs, this is a particularly good one in which to repurpose them!

NOTE

Put the extra pineapple to fruitful use, either fresh or frozen in 1-inch chunks, in pies like Squiggle Room (page 196) or Caught Off Shard (page 264).

RIGHTS OF FANCY

Dim sum is a type of Chinese cuisine that involves small plates of food offered to patrons on mobile carts. Weekend brunches with my grandparents often meant dining in this style, in which a multitude of dishes were always ordered. Regular items featured on our table included fried glutinous rice dumplings filled with meat (my favorite), radish cakes, pork buns, and chicken feet. And to conclude every meal, egg tarts—sweet, creamy custard cupped in flaky pastry, eaten in two or three avid chomps.

I've expanded the portions of the standard egg tart here and added a slate of strawberries to balance the sweetness of the custard and bring an extra dimension of color. It's a twist on a classic that makes it all that and dim sum.

1 fully baked Matcha Green Tea Tart Pastry Shell (page 35)

HONG KONG–STYLE EGG CUSTARD

1 cup (237 milliliters) boiling water

½ cup (99 grams) granulated sugar

2 large eggs plus 2 egg yolks

½ cup (118 milliliters) evaporated milk

¼ teaspoon kosher salt

1. Preheat the oven to 350°F.

2. Dissolve the sugar in the boiling water. Let the mixture cool to room temperature.

3. Combine the eggs, egg yolks, evaporated milk, and salt in a medium bowl and whisk until smooth. Mix in the sugar water. Strain the mixture through a fine-mesh sieve to eliminate any bubbles and large clumps of egg white.

4. Pour the egg mixture into the fully baked tart shell placed on a rimmed baking sheet. Gently poke away any remaining bubbles on the surface.

5. Carefully transfer the baking sheet to the oven and bake for 25 to 30 minutes, or until the custard is just set.

6. Cool completely before decorating.

STRAWBERRY RIGHT TRIANGLE DESIGN PROCESS

15 to 20 large fresh strawberries

1 green kiwi (optional)

1 × ½-inch rectangle cutter

Chef's knife

Ruler

1. Hull the strawberries and slice them in half, crown to point. Cut a rectangle out of each strawberry half with a 1-inch rectangle cutter or a chef's knife. Slice each rectangle in half on the diagonal to create two right triangles.

2. If using, peel and cut the kiwi into ¼-inch slices. Cut kiwi right triangles to match your strawberry shapes.

recipe continues

T
A
R
T

T
A
R
T

3. Lay a ruler, resting on the edges of the pan, horizontally across the center of the tart. Starting from the left edge of the tart, place a line of strawberry right triangles with the short edges parallel to the ruler. The triangles should be touching at the lower corners. If you're feeling brazen, toss a kiwi triangle into the mix.

4. Once the first row has been completed, lay another row of strawberry triangles directly above the first row. The lower corners of the triangles in this new row should touch the apexes of the triangles in the first row.

5. Continue laying lines of right triangles until the entire surface of the tart has been covered. If you like, randomly substitute a handful of kiwi triangles for strawberries to bring an abstract aesthetic to an otherwise precise pattern. Cut shapes to size as necessary at the edges of the tart.

6. Keep in the refrigerator until ready to serve. This tart is best consumed within 2 days.

SUGGESTED SUBSTITUTIONS

Crust alternative: Basic Tart Pastry Shell (page 31)

Topping alternatives: Mango, papaya, pineapple, kiwi, dragon fruit

NOTES

If your baked tart shell has any cracks, consider opting for a denser filling like the matcha white chocolate cheesecake (see page 78), as a liquid filling like this egg custard will leak through before becoming fully baked (page 22). Any strawberry scraps can be utilized fresh or frozen in pies like In It to Spin It (page 208), Kiss and Shell (page 217), or Sun in a Million (page 200).

LIFE OF THE TARTY

Since our little baby college years, Ben, my now-husband and perennial life of the party, has requested a lemon tart as his annual birthday treat. The creation I develop each March has evolved greatly over the years, but this one is perhaps the product that best straddles the line between what he sees as tradition and I view as an opportunity to riff. It retains the tart, citrus-y flavor profile he loves so much, and still gives me just enough room to party plan on my own terms, kiwi confetti and all. In fact, it's good enough to make him overlook the year the lemon tart resembled and tasted suspiciously like a batch of cinnamon rolls.

1 fully baked Basic Tart Pastry Shell (page 31)

LEMON BASIL CURD

1 cup (198 grams) granulated sugar

½ cup (1 ounce/28 grams) fresh basil leaves

Zest of 2 lemons

1 cup (237 milliliters) fresh lemon juice, from about 8 lemons

4 large eggs plus 4 egg yolks

½ teaspoon kosher salt

6 tablespoons (85 grams) unsalted butter, cut into ½-inch cubes

1. Preheat the oven to 350°F.

2. Combine the sugar, basil, and lemon zest in a food processor and blitz until the basil leaves have been completely incorporated into the sugar. Consider slathering yourself in this fragrant green sugar, but resist the urge and forge on.

3. Pour the sugar into a 2-quart saucepan. Add the lemon juice, eggs, egg yolks, and salt and whisk to combine. Cook over medium heat, stirring continuously, until the mixture is warmed through. Add the butter gradually and stir until all the cubes have melted. Continue cooking until the mixture is thick enough to coat a spatula, 5 to 8 minutes, stirring frequently and scraping the corners of the saucepan. Remove from the heat and strain the curd through a fine-mesh sieve.

4. Keep the baked tart shell in the tart pan and place it on a baking sheet. Pour the curd into the tart shell and smooth the surface.

5. Bake the tart for 5 to 10 minutes, just to set the filling. The edges should be solid while the center retains the slightest of jiggles.

6. Cool completely before decorating.

KIWI CONFETTI DESIGN PROCESS

2 firm-ripe green kiwis

Chef's knife

1. Peel the kiwis and cut them crosswise into ¼-inch slices. Cut the slices in half and cut each half into quarters or sixths.

2. Remove the tart from the pan and place it carefully on a plate.

3. Scoop all the kiwi triangles with both hands, shout "let's tarty!" and toss them up in the air to confetti over the tart. Admire where the kiwis land and the design that has resulted from the enthusiastic festivities. Kidding. Kind of. This is the simplest design in the book. Have a blast with it and take any approach you want—be it free-form improvisation or controlled mayhem! Arrange the kiwis in a scatter, rotating triangles every which way and sprinkling them randomly throughout the tart surface. Thrillingly, the cleanup on this party is a cinch. The only vacuum you'll need is your mouth.

4. Keep in the refrigerator until ready to serve. Then tarty hearty! This tart is best consumed within 2 days.

SUGGESTED SUBSTITUTIONS

Crust alternative: Matcha Green Tea Tart Pastry Shell (page 35)

Topping alternatives: Strawberry, dragon fruit, peach, plum

PIEOMETRY

TILE BY FIRE

My grandmother lives in Tegucigalpa, Honduras, where I spent the majority of my childhood summers. Some of my earliest memories include toddling about on the sun-drenched outdoor patio. As I grew older, those memories expanded to dancing and jump-roping and reading and then languishing moodily in all my teenage angst. The patio was also where I picked mangos, destroyed birthday piñatas, and slurped passion fruit juice by the gallon.

I always dreamed that I'd grow up to buy that house with its magical patio. I harbored grand plans to redo the tile, string a swath of twinkly lights, and live out the rest of my days in a haze of nostalgia and jugo de maracuyá. That path isn't looking likely, but the essence of that fantasy is captured in this tart. My favorite tropical flavors, my ideal geometric tile scheme, and all the warmth of a luminous childhood remembered.

1 baked Speculoos Cookie Crust (page 29)

PASSION FRUIT CURD

¾ cup (167 grams/ 6 ounces) passion fruit pulp, seeds removed

¾ cup (149 grams) granulated sugar

3 large eggs plus 3 egg yolks

1 teaspoon kosher salt

4 tablespoons (½ stick/57 grams) unsalted butter, at room temperature, cut into ½-inch cubes

1. Preheat the oven to 350°F.

2. Combine the passion fruit pulp, sugar, eggs, egg yolks, and salt in a 2-quart saucepan and whisk well. Cook over medium heat, whisking continuously, until the mixture is warmed through. Add the butter gradually and stir until all the cubes have melted. Continue cooking until the mixture is thick enough to coat a spatula, 5 to 8 minutes, stirring frequently and scraping the corners of the saucepan. Remove from the heat and strain the curd through a fine-mesh sieve.

3. Keep the baked tart shell in the tart pan and place on a baking sheet. Pour the curd into the tart shell and smooth the surface.

4. Bake the tart for 5 minutes, just to set the curd.

5. Cool completely before decorating.

SQUARE TILE DESIGN PROCESS

1 small ripe orange-fleshed papaya, such as Sunrise

1-inch square cutter

Paring knife

Ruler

1. Slice the papaya in half lengthwise and scoop out the seeds. Wrap one half and reserve for another use. Peel the other half and cut it crosswise into ¼-inch slices.

2. Using a 1-inch square cutter, punch out 50 squares of papaya. Snack on the scraps or freeze for future smoothies. Slice each square in half on the diagonal to make 100 triangles. Using one corner of the same 1-inch square cutter, cut out a

recipe continues

triangle from the hypotenuse (long side) of each right triangle. The result will be a V-shaped papaya piece and a tiny triangle. (Feel free to opt for a large square cutter if the size of these pieces is sheer insanity to you. While the technique for this design is not technically difficult, manipulating the fruit pieces into place may prove a true tile by fire for some—or a zen-like meditative practice for others.)

3. Place the tart on your work surface, keeping it in the tart pan. Lay a ruler horizontally across the center of the tart and resting on the edges of the tart pan.

4. Starting at the left edge of the tart, place a papaya V lining its two arms with the ruler. Because of the curved tart edge, the mirror image V to be placed underneath must be trimmed to fit. Do this now or return to it after the rest of the row has been laid.

5. Next, place two papaya Vs back-to-back, like a "greater than" symbol on the left and a "less than" symbol on the right. Now lay a small triangle, pointing outward, in the opening of each V.

6. The next fruit unit will be the same configuration but rotated 90 degrees. Continue placing papaya in this fashion until a row is completed.

7. The procedure for placing the next row of papaya is the same, but each unit in row 2 should be the quarter-turned image of its counterpart directly above. Continue placing papaya until the entire surface of the tart is covered, cutting pieces to size as necessary at row ends.

8. Keep in the refrigerator until ready to serve. This tart is best consumed within 2 days.

SUGGESTED SUBSTITUTIONS

Crust alternatives: Coconut Pecan Crust (page 30), Basic Tart Pastry Shell (page 31), Chocolate Tart Pastry Shell (page 32)

Topping alternatives: Mango, pineapple, kiwi, strawberry

NOTE
Utilize leftover papaya in another tart like Hex and Balances (page 81) and extra passion fruit puree in a pie like Sun in a Million (page 200).

TRUTH OR SQUARE

Growing up, anytime we drove by a Dairy Queen, my brother and I would lock eyes in the back seat and silently mime a flashing turn signal, willing the car to pull into the parking lot for Oreo blizzards. We never dared beg aloud, but that didn't stop us from hoping for a chance at the coveted treat. On the occasion that our parents would in fact surprise us, we'd break into triumphant chants, confident that it was our vigorous charade that manifested the victory into being.

This frosty number with its speckled Oreo crust and flurry of Andes mints is both a throwback to kiddie cravings and a coming-of-age celebration, because no parental consent is required here!

1 baked Funfetti Oreo Crust (page 28), cooled completely

ICE CREAM FILLING

3 cups (420 grams) mint chip ice cream, slightly softened

ANDES MINT TILE DESIGN PROCESS

40 Andes mint chocolates

Chef's knife

1. Keep the Oreo crust in the tart pan and scoop the softened ice cream into the prepared shell. Gently spread the ice cream and smooth the surface with an offset spatula. Chill the tart in the freezer while you prepare the topping.

2. Unwrap the Andes mints, taking care not to smudge the smooth side of the chocolate with fingerprints. Place each chocolate logo-side down and use a sharp chef's knife to cut each mint crosswise down the middle to create two equal squares. If a piece of chocolate cracks and splinters into another shape, pop it in your mouth and cut another mint. In general, room-temperature chocolate slices best here.

3. Remove the chilled tart from the freezer. Lay a ruler horizontally across the tart, 1 inch from the top. Starting from

recipe continues

the left, place one square of chocolate, aligning the bottom edge of the square with the ruler. Place another square of chocolate, rotated 45 degrees, next to the first square. The corner of the second square should touch the side of the first square. Repeat this process, alternating the angles of the squares, until the row has been completed. You may need to cut a square to size, depending on the remaining space at the end of the row.

4. Move the ruler down 1 inch, maintaining a horizontal line. Place a rotated square of chocolate directly under the first piece of chocolate in the first row. The top corner of the square should touch the bottom side of the first square. Continue this process until the row has been filled. Repeat row by row until the entire surface of the tart has been covered.

5. Wrap well and keep this tart in the freezer for up to a week. Let the tart sit on the counter for several minutes after removing from the freezer, then cut with a chef's knife.

SUGGESTED SUBSTITUTIONS

Crust alternative: Speculoos Cookie Crust (page 29)

Filling alternatives: Substitute any ice cream flavor of choice!

MOST VALUABLE LAYER

Once upon an era past, I had an all-encompassing obsession with dinosaurs. In kindergarten, I was certain I wanted to spend my life digging up *Tyrannosaurus rex* bones and told my teacher I was going to rule The Land Before Time. Ultimately, those aspirations were obliterated by an unforeseen meteor and doomed to prehistoric lore, but I did manage to pivot to a niche area of study known as pieleontology. Refer to exhibit A, displaying the effects of evolution on the Coconut Age and the White and Dark Chocolate Ages perfectly preserved in the bedrock of matcha. Imfossibly fascinating stuff!

1 fully baked Matcha Green Tea Tart Pastry Shell (page 35), cooled completely

NO-BAKE MATCHA WHITE CHOCOLATE CHEESECAKE

8 ounces (227 grams) white chocolate, finely chopped

2 tablespoons (12 grams) matcha green tea powder (see page 16)

1 cup (237 milliliters) heavy cream

8 ounces (227 grams) cream cheese, at room temperature

1. Microwave the white chocolate in a microwave-safe bowl, stopping to stir every 30 seconds, until melted and smooth. Sift in the matcha powder and stir to incorporate. Let cool to room temperature.

2. Put the heavy cream in a medium bowl and whip with an electric mixer on high to soft peaks. Set aside.

3. In a large bowl, whip the cream cheese with an electric mixer on medium speed until smooth and creamy. Add the cooled matcha and white chocolate mixture and beat on medium-high until fluffy, about 2 minutes. With the mixer on low, beat in half of the whipped cream. Gently fold in the remaining whipped cream with a spatula until just combined. Do not overmix.

4. Scoop the filling into the prepared matcha tart shell and smooth the surface with an offset spatula. Store the tart in the refrigerator until ready to serve.

TEXTURED LAYERS DESIGN PROCESS

½ cup (60 grams) unsweetened coconut chips

2 ounces (56 grams) white chocolate

2 ounces (56 grams) dark chocolate

Toothpick or paring knife

Chef's knife

1. Put ¼ cup (30 grams) of the coconut chips in a small skillet and toast over medium heat until golden, stirring frequently.

2. Depending on your desired texture, shave, grate, or finely chop the chocolates, keeping them separate.

3. Using a toothpick or the tip of a paring knife, lightly draw wavy lines with approximately 1 inch of separation across the surface of the matcha cheesecake to create an abstract layer design. Fill in the various layers with the untoasted coconut, toasted coconut, white chocolate, and dark chocolate, alternating among the toppings and leaving some layers empty to let the green filling show through. A toothpick or the tip of the paring knife can be used to nudge errant coconut chips or chocolate bits into place.

4. Keep in the refrigerator until ready to serve. This tart is best consumed within 2 days.

SUGGESTED SUBSTITUTIONS

Crust alternatives: Coconut Pecan Crust (page 30), Basic Tart Pastry Shell (page 31), Chocolate Tart Pastry Shell (page 32)

Topping alternatives: Chopped nuts, sprinkles, Oreo crumbs

HEX AND BALANCES

The first time I caught a whiff of traditional green spirulina (a nutrient-rich algae), I gagged and the container slipped from my hand, causing the powder to violently mushroom cloud and dust my kitchen surfaces with its stench. The distilled blue stuff called for below is not only far less offensive, but it also tints the lemon curd a glorious teal shade, which contrasts happily with the bright hues of papaya and pink dragon fruit. With a coconut crust also in play, this tart is the tropical island of desserts, and just looking at it makes me want to throw on a swimsuit and dive right into the sea.

1 baked Coconut Pecan Crust (page 30)

SPIRULINA LEMON CURD

1 cup (198 grams) granulated sugar

1 teaspoon blue spirulina powder (see page 16; optional; see Notes)

1 teaspoon kosher salt

1 cup (237 milliliters) fresh lemon juice, from about 6 lemons

4 eggs plus 2 egg yolks

4 tablespoons (½ stick/57 grams) unsalted butter, cut into ½-inch cubes

1. Preheat the oven to 350°F.

2. Combine the sugar, spirulina powder, and salt in a 2-quart saucepan and whisk until no lumps remain. Add the lemon juice, eggs, and egg yolks and whisk to combine. Cook over medium heat, whisking continuously, until the mixture is warmed through. Add the butter gradually and stir until all the cubes have melted. Continue cooking until the mixture is thick enough to coat a spatula, 5 to 8 minutes, stirring frequently and scraping the corners of the saucepan. Remove from the heat and strain the curd through a fine-mesh sieve.

3. Keep the baked tart shell in the pan and place it on a baking sheet. Pour the curd into the tart shell and smooth the surface.

4. Bake the tart for 5 minutes, just to set the curd.

5. Cool completely before decorating.

TESSELLATED TRAPEZOID DESIGN PROCESS

1 small ripe orange-fleshed papaya, such as Sunrise

1 pink-fleshed dragon fruit (pitaya)

1-inch hexagon cutter

Paring knife

1. Slice the papaya in half lengthwise and scoop out the seeds. Wrap one half and reserve for another tart, such as Tile by Fire (page 71). Peel the other half and cut it crosswise into ¼-inch slices. Using a 1-inch hexagon cutter, punch out 30 hexagons. Cut each hexagon in half, point to point, to create two identical trapezoids.

2. Trim and peel the dragon fruit and cut it into ¼-inch slices. Using the 1-inch hexagon cutter, punch out 30 hexagons. Cut

each hexagon in half, point to point, to create two identical trapezoids.

3. Starting from the top left of the tart, place a papaya trapezoid with its longest edge on the bottom.

4. Next, place a dragon fruit trapezoid such that its top right corner touches the bottom left corner of the papaya trapezoid. This dragon fruit piece should also align with the left edge of the tart. Place another dragon fruit trapezoid with its top left corner touching the bottom right corner of the first papaya piece.

5. To avoid staining the papaya with bright pink juice, wipe your fingers after placing each dragon fruit piece. Place another papaya trapezoid in the same row as the first papaya piece, touching its bottom left corner to the top right corner of the dragon fruit trapezoid. Continue alternating placement of dragon fruit and papaya trapezoids in their respective rows.

6. When these two rows have been completed, continue moving down the surface of the tart, laying two rows of fruit at a time, alternating between papaya and dragon fruit, to create a full trapezoid tessellation.

7. Keep in the refrigerator until ready to serve. This tart is best consumed within 2 days.

SUGGESTED SUBSTITUTIONS

Crust alternatives: Speculoos Cookie Crust (page 29), Basic Tart Pastry Shell (page 31)

Topping alternatives: Mango, white-fleshed dragon fruit, kiwi, strawberry

NOTES

Blue spirulina can be quite pricy, so feel free to omit. Note that skipping the spirulina will result in a basic yellow lemon curd.

Pink dragon fruit can be very juicy. If you're concerned about staining your fingers, wear food-grade disposable gloves. Leftover pink dragon fruit can be juiced, strained, and used as a substitute for water in the Dragon Fruit Pie Dough (page 155).

LIVIN' ON A PAIR

When Ben and I moved to Seattle, we drove from Boston and the road trip was a comedy of errors. Our AC gave out early on in the journey, and the scorching stretch through Montana in mid-August nearly incinerated us. The car was jammed with our belongings, so we could only crack the windows, merely switching the oven to convection mode.

Under normal circumstances, the copilot oversees DJ duties and snack dispersal. In this instance, however, whoever was in the passenger seat had to regularly revive the driver with two ice packs to the face from our dinky cooler of drinks.

To keep from passing out, we fantasized about smoothies and sorbet and Popsicles and endless varieties of ice-cold lemonade. It was only by the sheer force of a citrus-fueled trance and teamwork that we made it to Seattle that summer.

This tart, with its lemon-driven flavor profile and complementary pairings, is the only way I'll tolerate reliving that misadventure. But boy, is it a trip!

1 baked Coconut Pecan Crust (page 30)

TWO-TONED LEMON CURD SWIRL

½ recipe spirulina lemon curd (see page 81)

½ recipe pink lemonade curd (see page 48)

1. Preheat the oven to 350°F.

2. Prepare a half recipe of the spirulina lemon curd and a half recipe of the pink lemonade curd, separating them in two small bowls.

3. Tear off a 12-inch square of aluminum foil. Fold 2 inches along one side, then fold that section over another 2 inches. Continue folding until you have a 2 × 12-inch band. Shape it into your desired curve(s), and stand it in the prepared tart shell like a dividing wall.

4. Using one hand to hold the foil in place, slowly pour or spoon the pink lemonade curd into one section, starting from the outer edge of the tart. Slow when the curd begins to approach but does not touch the foil divider.

5. Pour the spirulina lemon curd into the other section, slowing as the curd reaches the foil. Carefully fill in and smooth the curds on their respective sides, continuing to hold the divider in place, until each section has been filled to the center. Gently lift the divider straight up, rinse it, and recycle it.

6. Place the tart on a rimmed baking sheet and bake for 5 minutes, just to set the filling. The edges should be set with the center retaining the slightest of jiggles.

7. Cool completely before decorating.

PAIRED SPHERES DESIGN PROCESS

4 firm green kiwis

1 white-fleshed dragon fruit (pitaya)

1-inch circle cutter

Paring knife

Ruler

1. Peel the kiwis and cut them crosswise into ¼-inch slices. Using a 1-inch circle cutter, punch out 20 kiwi circles. Cut each circle in half to create 40 half-moon shapes.

2. Peel the dragon fruit and cut it crosswise into ¼-inch slices. Using a 1-inch circle cutter, punch out 20 dragon fruit circles. Cut each circle in half to create 40 half-moon shapes.

recipe continues

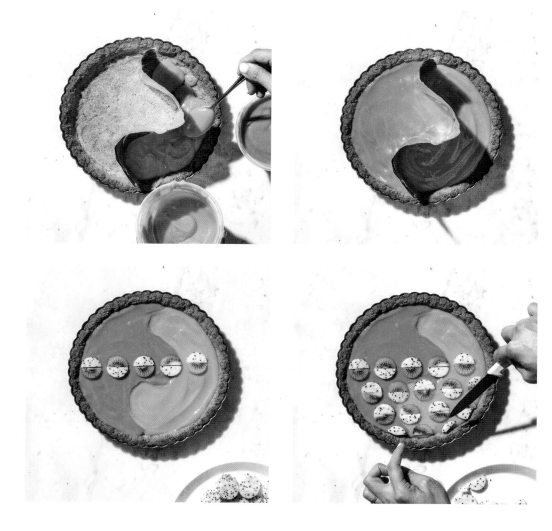

3. Lay a ruler horizontally across the center of the tart. Starting from the left, place a row of semicircles with the straight edge against the ruler, alternating between dragon fruit and kiwi. Remove the ruler and complete each circle with its opposite fruit, pairing dragon fruit with kiwi and vice versa.

4. When the first row has been completed, repeat the same process. Continue filling rows of kiwi and dragon fruit circles until the surface of the tart has been evenly covered, trimming edge pieces to fit as necessary.

5. Keep in the refrigerator until ready to serve. This tart is best consumed within 2 days.

SUGGESTED SUBSTITUTIONS

Crust alternatives: Speculoos Cookie Crust (page 29), Basic Tart Pastry Shell (page 31)

Topping alternatives: Mango, pink-fleshed dragon fruit, pineapple, papaya, strawberry

NOTES

Since shape cutters are not particularly sharp, swiveling the cutter on the kiwi slices can be a better alternative to pushing straight down and running the risk of smashed fruit.

As a design variation, create a layered curd tart instead of the side-by-side swirl. Pour the spirulina lemon curd into the prepared tart shell and spread into an even layer. Chill in the refrigerator for 10 minutes to set until it no longer jiggles. Gently spoon the pink lemonade curd over the spirulina layer and smooth the top. Bake at 350°F for 5 minutes, just to set the curd. Decorate, chill in the refrigerator, then slice to reveal the stacked duo tones.

BERRIED TREASURE

I have an uncanny ability to conjure inclement weather everywhere I go. The first time I traveled to Portland to meet Ben's parents, there was a catastrophic ice storm and I had to wear his mother's clothes all week. My first winter in Boston brought the worst snowstorm in history, with 109 inches of the horrible white stuff and a hideous poop-colored parka I cowered in for months. When we finally fled back west, everyone reassured me that it never snows in Seattle. Guess what? It has snowed all three years. *Rude.*

I'm a July baby, born and raised in glorious San Diego, California. I live for summer, and I'm pretty sure sunshine burns through my veins. This tart, with its breezy lavender cream and vibrant berry ombré, is the antithesis of the woolly winters that torment me. It is farmers' markets bursting with peak summer produce, air perfumed with barbecue char, and dinner out on the patio every single night. Make it at the height of berry season as the crown glory to any outdoor picnic. Or unearth this treasure in chillier months to remind yourself that it's always sunny somewhere . . . and for a moment, that somewhere could be your kitchen.

Please note that this recipe requires an overnight step before assembly!

1 baked Basic Shortbread Crust (page 26), cooled completely

LAVENDER BLACKBERRY WHIPPED CREAM

2 teaspoons dried food-grade lavender

1 cup (237 milliliters) heavy cream

½ cup (3 ounces/85 grams) fresh blackberries

8 ounces (225 grams) cream cheese

1 cup (113 grams) powdered sugar

¼ teaspoon kosher salt

PREPARE A DAY AHEAD

1. Combine the lavender and heavy cream in a small saucepan. Heat over medium-low just until steam lifts off the surface and a tiny line of bubbles forms around the edge. Do not let the cream boil. Chill in the refrigerator overnight or until cold.

DAY OF

2. Strain the cream and discard the lavender. In a large bowl with an electric mixer, whip the cold lavender-infused cream to soft peaks. Set aside.

3. Puree the blackberries and scrape the mixture through a fine-mesh sieve with a spatula to extract as much pulp as possible. You should have slightly less than ¼ cup (59 milliliters) puree. Discard the remaining seeds and set the puree aside.

4. In a large bowl, combine the cream cheese, powdered sugar, and salt. Blend with an electric mixer on medium speed until smooth. Add the blackberry puree and mix on medium speed until well combined. Gently fold in the whipped cream with a spatula. Do not overmix.

TART
TART

BERRY OMBRÉ DESIGN PROCESS

5 cups (20 ounces/567 grams) assorted fresh berries

1. Remove the baked and cooled shortbread crust from the pan and place it carefully on a plate. Dollop the blackberry whipped cream in the center and use an offset spatula to swoop and swirl the cream outward, leaving a ¼-inch edge of exposed crust.

2. Arrange the berries on your work surface by hue from darkest to lightest. Depending on how many different colors you have, mentally divide the tart in as many sections.

3. Starting from the left edge of the tart, fill a vertical section with the darkest berries. For extra dimension, mound the berries by stacking some as a jumble on top. Transition to the next darkest berry, again filling a vertical column. Continue moving across the surface of the tart, placing fruit in columns, ending with the lightest color.

4. Keep in the refrigerator until ready to serve. This tart is best consumed the day it is made.

SUGGESTED SUBSTITUTIONS

Crust alternatives: Basic Tart Pastry Shell (page 31), Chocolate Tart Pastry Shell (page 32), Chocolate Matcha Shortbread Crust (page 27)

Topping alternatives: While they may not give the same ombré effect, most fruits (with the exception of citrus) pair well with this tart.

NOTE

As a design variation, build the berry ombré radially. Arrange the lightest colored berries in a circle in the center of the tart and continue moving outward in rings, transitioning from lightest to darkest.

HEADS OR SCALES

My paternal grandfather had an entire wall of aquariums in his house. Every Sunday, I'd check the fridge for 7Up (because that didn't exist at our house!) and then take my soda to the back room. I spent myriad hours doing nothing but sitting on the floor sipping my bubbly and watching fish swim infinite loops around their tanks with the gurgling of the filters as a gentle soundtrack to those afternoons. There are so many significant things, like birth dates or anniversaries, that I can barely remember, but I vividly recall these otherwise unremarkable afternoons.

When I posted a tart similar to this one on Instagram, it got a huge response. I was surprised because of the design's simplicity, but, like memories, sometimes the most quotidian are the ones that stay with us.

1 baked Speculoos Cookie Crust (page 29)

BLUEBERRY MINT CURD

2 cups (12 ounces/340 grams) fresh or frozen blueberries

½ cup (99 grams) granulated sugar

4 large fresh mint leaves

Zest of 1 lemon

¼ cup (59 milliliters) fresh lemon juice

2 large eggs plus 2 egg yolks

¼ teaspoon kosher salt

4 tablespoons (½ stick/57 grams) unsalted butter, cut into ½-inch cubes

1. Preheat the oven to 350°F.

2. Combine the blueberries and 1 tablespoon water in a 2-quart saucepan. Cook over medium heat, stirring occasionally, until the berries burst and start to break down, about 10 minutes. Using a silicone spatula, press the berries through a fine-mesh sieve, extracting as much puree as possible. Scrape the puree back into the saucepan and discard the pulp. Set aside.

3. Blitz the sugar, mint, and lemon zest in a food processor until no large pieces of mint remain. Uncover the food processor, inhale deeply, and pause for a brief moment of aromatherapy.

4. Pour the lemon mint sugar into the saucepan with the blueberry puree. Add the lemon juice, eggs, egg yolks, and salt and whisk well. Cook over medium heat, stirring continuously, until the mixture is warmed through. Add the butter gradually and stir until all the cubes have melted. Continue cooking until the mixture is thick enough to coat a spatula, 5 to 8 minutes, stirring frequently and scraping the corners of the saucepan.

5. Remove from the heat and strain the curd through the fine-mesh sieve.

6. Keep the tart shell in the tart pan and place it on a baking sheet. Pour the curd into the tart shell, smoothing the surface.

7. Bake the tart for 5 minutes, just to set the filling.

8. Cool completely before decorating.

KIWI SCALE DESIGN PROCESS

2 or 3 firm green kiwis

2 or 3 firm golden kiwis

1-inch circle cutter

Paring knife

Ruler

1. Peel the kiwis and cut crosswise into ⅛-inch slices. Using a 1-inch circle cutter, punch out 36 shapes from the kiwi slices. Cut each kiwi circle in half to produce two identical semicircles.

2. Lay a ruler horizontally across the tart, ½ inch below the top edge. Starting from the left, place a golden kiwi semicircle on the surface, aligning the straight edge with the ruler. Next, place a green kiwi semicircle adjacent to the first kiwi, also aligning the straight edge with the ruler. Continue placing kiwi pieces in a line, alternating between gold and green, until the entire row has been completed. You may need to cut the kiwi pieces down to size to fit the remaining space at the end of the row.

3. Move the ruler ½ inch below the first line of kiwis to use as a reference for row 2. Place a golden kiwi semicircle such that the center of the round edge touches the point where two semicircles in row 1 meet. The straight edge of the newly placed kiwi piece should still align with the ruler. Continue placing kiwis in this fashion, alternating between green and gold, to complete the second row. Move the ruler ½ inch below each kiwi line to set up for the next row. Repeat the process until the entire surface of the tart has been covered.

4. Keep in the refrigerator until ready to serve. This tart is best consumed within 2 days.

SUGGESTED SUBSTITUTIONS

Crust alternatives: Coconut Pecan Crust (page 30), Basic Tart Pastry Shell (page 31)

Topping alternatives: Mango, papaya, pineapple, dragon fruit, strawberry

NOTE

Snack on the kiwi scraps or freeze for future smoothies!

THE SECRET INGRADIENT

My family came to visit at the end of my year abroad in Spain, and we took a road trip that led us to Logroño for a few nights. We were deep in Rioja wine country with a million cobblestone streets to traverse and pintxos to consume, but my dad was most content lounging in the yard of our rental, picking and eating cherries right off the tree. It's an enduring image of simplicity and bliss—mild sunshine and my father at the picnic table with handfuls of fruit and the biggest grin on his face.

Cherries always hold this feeling of quiet euphoria for me now, and their short season is always a reminder to indulge in meaningful moments. Whether extravagant milestones or serene seconds, the secret is to cherrysh them.

In that vein, I've included two variations for this ombré design—one simple and another even more so. Whatever your path, choose the one that Bings you joy.

1 fully baked Matcha Green Tea Tart Pastry Shell (page 35), cooled completely

BLACK SESAME WHITE CHOCOLATE MOUSSE

8 ounces (228 grams) white chocolate, finely chopped

1 tablespoon black tahini (see page 13)

¼ teaspoon kosher salt

½ cup (120 milliliters) heavy cream

1. Put the white chocolate in a heatproof medium bowl and heat it in the microwave, stirring every 30 seconds, until the chocolate is completely melted and smooth. Add the black tahini and salt and stir until well combined. Set aside to cool to room temperature.

2. In a separate medium bowl, whip the heavy cream to soft peaks. Gently fold the whipped cream into the cooled black sesame–white chocolate mixture until just combined. Do not overmix. Scoop the mousse into the baked and cooled tart shell and smooth the surface with an offset spatula.

3. Chill the tart in the refrigerator while you prepare the fruit for decoration.

T
A
R
T
A
R
T

OMBRÉ MOSAIC DESIGN PROCESS

20 fresh yellow-blush cherries, such as Rainier, pitted

20 fresh red cherries, such as Bing, pitted

Chef's knife

1. Set out three plates on a work surface. It's helpful to organize cherry pieces by color as you cut them, so designate one plate for the darkest shades, one for bright red shades, and one for yellow and blush shades.

2. Cut each cherry in half, stem to tail. If a cherry is duo-toned (for example, some Rainier cherries are half blush, half yellow), try to cut along the color line so you have two solid-colored halves. Trim off the stem edge and the bottom edge of each cherry half to create a rectangle with clean lines (see Note). File each cherry piece on the appropriate plate according to its color. Collect all the cherry trimmings in a small pile until you've amassed a juicy handful to shovel down your gullet. Cherry season is short. There is no time to waste on decorum.

3. Remove the tart from the refrigerator. Starting at the bottom edge of the tart, arrange dark, maroon-colored cherry pieces in a tightly scattered configuration. The beauty of a mosaic-style design is that the individual pieces need not be lined perfectly and precisely in rows. Instead, you can place one piece horizontally, the next diagonally, the next vertically, and so forth. Cover a section approximately 2 inches wide with the darkest-colored cherry pieces, gradually transitioning to cherries that are shades of bright red.

4. Continue placing cherry pieces in an arrangement of controlled chaos, gradually transitioning to lighter and brighter shades. The profusion of color should gradate from dark red to yellow as you traverse the surface of the tart.

5. Keep the tart in the refrigerator until ready to serve. This tart is best consumed the day it is made.

NOTE

For an easier ombré design, simply slice the cherries in half, stem to tail. Arrange the cherry halves on the tart in horizontal rows, lining the bottom of the tart with the darkest cherries and gradually transitioning to lighter shades as you move up the surface.

SUGGESTED SUBSTITUTIONS

Crust alternative: Basic Tart Pastry Shell (page 31)

Topping alternatives: Raspberries, plums, or apricots of varying colors

PLAY TO FIN

I'm no morning person, but being with Ben often means dawn patrol. When we lived in Southern California, we would schlep a slew of towels, a surfboard, and one supremely stinky wetsuit and drive down the coastline, surveying the surf until we found an acceptable swell. If a set passed muster, we'd haul everything down to the sand, and Ben would jog out to brave the frigid water for several hours. Meanwhile, my bed head and I would beach ourselves on dry land with a paperback to pass time until the post-surf beeline to breakfast burritos.

I always harbored a latent affection for those sessions by the sea and now that we no longer live within driving distance of surfable waves, I really miss those briny-scented mornings. Hopefully we'll move back to California one day, but until then, I'll content myself with these little plum fins that remind me so much of overturned surfboards on the shore, against a backdrop of sea foam, drying off before the happy trek back to the car.

1 baked Chocolate Matcha Shortbread Crust (page 27), cooled completely

SWEET CREAM FILLING
8 ounces (225 grams) cream cheese, at room temperature

½ cup (99 grams) granulated sugar

Combine the cream cheese and sugar in a medium bowl and blend with an electric mixer until smooth.

PLUM FIN DESIGN PROCESS

5 firm plums

Chef's knife

1. Halve and pit the plums. Place each plum half cut side down and slice each one into 8 pieces. One plum should yield 16 thin wedges.

2. Cut each plum slice in half crosswise to create a shark fin shape. Set aside.

3. Remove the baked and cooled shortbread crust from the pan and place it carefully on a plate. Dollop the sweet cream cheese in the center of the crust and spread it evenly over the surface of the crust with an offset spatula, leaving a ¼-inch edge of exposed crust.

4. Starting in the center of the top edge of your tart, stand a plum fin with the tip of the fin pointing to the left. Gently press the fin into the sweet cream cheese to secure. Place another fin directly below the first fin, but this time point the tip to the right. Continue placing the plum fins in a line down the center of the tart, alternating the direction of the tip each time.

5. Starting again at the top of the tart, but to the right of the center column, insert a plum fin pointing to the right. Place another fin pointing left directly below. Continue until the entire column has been completed. Repeat the process until the entire surface of the tart has been covered.

6. Keep the tart in the refrigerator until ready to serve. This tart is best consumed the day it is made.

SUGGESTED SUBSTITUTIONS

Crust alternative: Basic Tart Pastry Shell (page 31)

Topping alternatives: Apricot, pluot

NOTE

This design is difficult to execute with very ripe fruit. If your plums are soft, I recommend a pie like Seeing Is Beweaving (page 247) instead. Ensuring that your fruit is firm will make slicing a thousand times easier, and who couldn't do with one less headache?

NO RINGS ATTACHED

I have a friend who will order the lox and bagel platter at any brunch and spend the rest of the morning painstakingly constructing the perfect mouthful—bagel, cream cheese, salmon, tomato, red onion, and capers—with each and every bite. It's an admirable commitment to quality control, and one that's generally lost on the rest of us heathens who snarfle up our meals with a single inhale. My post-brunch plans usually center around a lengthy nap, so there is never a moment to lose when sleep is at stake. This masterpiece is a model of Sunday morning efficiency, where all the perfect bites are assembled in one go, leaving you plenty of afternoon for that leisurely snooze.

1 fully baked Everything (but the) Bagel Tart Pastry Shell (page 36), cooled completely

SMOKED SALMON CREAM CHEESE FILLING

8 ounces (225 grams) cream cheese

½ cup (125 grams) plain Greek yogurt

4 ounces (125 grams) smoked salmon, finely chopped

2 tablespoons minced red onion

1 tablespoon fresh lemon juice

1 tablespoon capers

1 tablespoon minced fresh dill

1 tablespoon minced fresh chives

1 teaspoon horseradish cream

½ teaspoon kosher salt

¼ teaspoon freshly ground black pepper

1. Combine the cream cheese and yogurt in a medium bowl and blend with an electric mixer until smooth. Add the remaining ingredients and stir with a spatula until well combined.

2. Spread the filling in the baked and cooled tart shell and smooth the surface.

10 ounces (280 grams) baby heirloom tomatoes in assorted colors

Paring knife

1. It's helpful to organize the tomatoes by color as you cut them, so set out three plates and designate one plate for dark purple tomatoes, one for red tomatoes, and one for orange ones.

2. Trim off the stem tops of the tomatoes. Cut the tomatoes crosswise into ¼-inch slices. File the tomato slices on the appropriate plates according to color.

3. Beginning with the darkest ones, arrange the tomato rings in an overlapping line around the outermost edge of the tart. Take care not to rest the tomatoes past the filling edge to avoid soggifying the crust.

4. Add the word *soggifying* to your culinary vocabulary.

5. When this first ring of tomatoes has been created, arrange an overlapping line of red tomatoes inside the purple ring. Complete the design by arranging a line of overlapping orange tomato slices to fill the center.

6. Serve immediately.

SUGGESTED SUBSTITUTIONS

Crust alternative: Herbed Tart Pastry Shell (page 38)

Topping alternatives: Red, white, and Easter egg radishes

NOTE

For a simpler ombré, slice the baby tomatoes in half. Arrange the tomatoes cut-side down and by color in concentric rings without overlap.

PIEOMETRY

WAVE OF WONDERS

As a lifelong San Diego Padres fan, I grew up in the illustrious heyday of Tony Gwynn and Trevor Hoffman. I used to enter poetry contests sponsored by the local supermarket to win baseball game tickets, and then I'd scream my little heart out from the nosebleed section for love of the game and free admission.

In addition to the soft serve in a helmet and the seventh-inning stretch, doing the wave was a major highlight. I was always amazed that so many people scattered around a stadium could coordinate a movement so fluid, even when some individuals weren't perfectly in sync.

This design, made up of many thin slices of fruit layered together, reminds me of that orchestrated effort. Even if some of your slices are a little thicker than others, or the placement of your rows a tad wobbly, the overall effect will still elicit wave reviews.

1 baked Basic Shortbread Crust (page 26), cooled completely

SPICED COFFEE CREAM

½ cup (118 milliliters) heavy cream

8 ounces (225 grams) cream cheese

½ cup (57 grams) powdered sugar

½ teaspoon ground cardamom

½ teaspoon ground cinnamon

¼ teaspoon kosher salt

¼ cup (59 milliliters) brewed black coffee, cold

1. In a medium bowl, whip the heavy cream to soft peaks with an electric mixer. Set aside.

2. Combine the cream cheese, powdered sugar, cardamom, cinnamon, and salt in a large bowl. Beat with the electric mixer until the mixture is smooth and no lumps remain, about 1 minute. Add the coffee 1 tablespoon at a time, mixing well after each addition.

3. Gently fold in the whipped cream until just incorporated. Set aside.

WAVY LAYER DESIGN PROCESS

1 firm red pear, such as D'Anjou

1 firm green pear, such as Concorde

1 firm yellow pear, such as Bartlett

1 firm brown pear, such as Bosc

Chef's knife or mandoline slicer

1. Stand the pears stem-up and run your knife straight down to cut each into four wedges, slicing as close to the core as possible but avoiding the seeds. It's okay if the sections vary in height, as this will lend an additional textural dimension to the tart.

2. Place each pear section skin-side up and cut into 1-millimeter slices. If you have a mandoline, this is a pearfect opportunity to use it, but watch your fingers! You'll need those

recipe continues

for this design (and every other one in the book, for that matter). The slices shouldn't be too thick to bend, but neither should they be so thin that they are translucent. They should retain enough structure to stand upright in the cream. Keep the pear slices organized by color as you slice.

3. Remove the baked and cooled shortbread crust from the pan and place it securely on a plate. Dollop the coffee cream in the center and spread it evenly over the surface of the crust with an offset spatula, leaving a ¼-inch edge of exposed crust.

4. Gather 8 pear slices of one color and lay them on their side in a slightly overlapping line on the cutting board. Carefully transfer the line of pears as a single unit and stand them skin side up in the coffee cream, curving the line slightly and using the cream to hold everything in place.

5. Gather 8 slices of another color and repeat the process of organizing them in an overlapping line. Transfer this group of slices to the tart and place it adjacent to the first line of fruit, following the curve. Continue this process of fitting lines of pears—staggering the lines, varying the curves, and alternating colors—until the entire surface of the tart has been covered. You can also vary the number of slices in each line of fruit depending on the remaining space.

6. This tart is most visually striking when served immediately. Refrigerated leftovers after the first day will still be tasty but less appealing in presentation, as the pear slices will brown.

SUGGESTED SUBSTITUTION

Topping alternative: Apples

NOTES

The type of pear matters less than the color variety, although for design variation, you can opt to limit your color assortment.

I serve this tart right away, but if you are concerned about oxidation, mix 2 tablespoons honey in a bowl with 1 cup water and soak the pear slices for 1 minute. Drain the slices and pat dry before arranging.

I love the idea of surprises, but I don't handle them well in execution. This especially applies to Christmas presents. If there are any wrapped gifts with my name on them remotely near a tree, *I must know what's inside immediately*. While this is not scientifically proven, I can anecdotally say that the suspense could actually kill me.

The first year we were married, I wore Ben down by requesting to open presents every day until he relented . . . a whole week before Christmas. Because we are adults and we do what we want (or because I have the patience of a five-year-old and Ben is only willing to bear my entreaties for so long), opening gifts early has since become an annual tradition.

This tart hits the sweet spot in that it holds all the delight of an exciting gift but harbors no surprises. All its jewels are on full display, and there is no escaping the spicy scent of the gingerbread caramel. But just to be safe . . . make this and unwrap it immediately.

1 baked Basic Shortbread Crust (page 26), cooled completely

GINGERBREAD CARAMEL

1 cup (198 grams) granulated sugar

2 tablespoons (43 grams) unsulphured molasses (see page 17)

1 teaspoon ground ginger

¾ teaspoon ground cinnamon

¼ teaspoon ground allspice

¼ teaspoon ground cloves

½ teaspoon kosher salt

¼ teaspoon freshly ground black pepper

2 tablespoons (28 grams) unsalted butter, cut into ½-inch cubes

1 cup (237 milliliters) heavy cream

1. Whisk the sugar, ½ cup (118 milliliters) water, and the molasses in a heavy-bottomed saucepan and bring to a boil over medium heat.

2. While waiting for the sugar and molasses to boil, whisk the ginger, cinnamon, allspice, cloves, salt, and pepper together in a small bowl. Set aside.

3. When the sugar and molasses mixture registers 250°F on a candy thermometer, remove from the heat. Add the butter and carefully whisk in the heavy cream. If the caramel seizes, return to low heat and whisk until smooth. Whisk in the spices. Cool completely and keep in the refrigerator until ready to use.

GINGERBREAD CARAMEL CREAM

8 ounces (225 grams) cream cheese, at room temperature

½ cup (6 ounces) gingerbread caramel

Combine the cream cheese and caramel in a mixing bowl. Blend with an electric mixer until smooth.

JEWEL BOX DESIGN PROCESS

6 figs

½ cup pomegranate arils

Paring knife

Toothpick

Tweezers

1. Trim the figs and cut them crosswise into ⅛-inch slices, discarding the ends. Cut each fig slice in half, and each half into 2 or 3 small wedges. Set aside.

2. Remove the baked and cooled shortbread crust from the pan and place it carefully on a plate. Dollop the gingerbread caramel cream in the center and spread it evenly over the

recipe continues

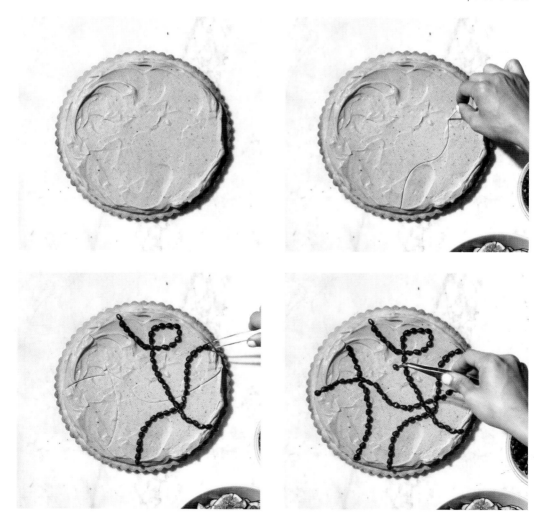

surface of the crust with an offset spatula, leaving a ¼-inch edge of exposed crust.

3. Use a toothpick to draw a wandering, curvy line in the cream across the middle of the tart. Draw another undulating line that intersects with the first line. Trace several more lines, spacing them out over the surface of the tart, adding smaller connecting squiggles as desired.

4. Pave the lines with pomegranate arils.

5. Fill in all the negative space between the pomegranate lines with fig wedges nestled tightly together. Since the tiny fig wedges can be difficult to maneuver, I like to scoop up each piece with the tip of my paring knife and then gently nudge it off the knife and onto the surface of the tart with my finger. Continue filling in fig wedges until the surface of the tart is completely covered and the gingerbread caramel cream is no longer visible.

6. Keep in the refrigerator until ready to serve. This tart is best consumed within 2 days.

SUGGESTED SUBSTITUTIONS

Topping alternatives: Pomegranate and green apple, blueberry and strawberry

NOTE

The gingerbread caramel yields 1 cup total, and this recipe uses ½ cup. Those who are seriously committed to their sweet tooth will slurp up the extra gingerbread caramel by the spoonful, but the All Strings Considered apple pie (page 213) is a solid backup plan!

SURVIVAL OF THE KNITTEST

I love luxuriating in big chunky knits, but I don't sew or crochet and I definitely can't knit, so this is the closest I'll come to fashioning any sort of cozy sweater with my own two hands. Rows of apples snuggle together on a bed of peanut butter mousse that's as soft as cashmere, and the flecks of color in the crust elevate the entire ensemble from frumpy pullover to hip thrifted vintage gem. With no risk of needle jabs or itchy wool, this tart is by far the sweater option.

1 baked Funfetti Oreo Crust (page 28), cooled

PEANUT BUTTER MOUSSE

1 cup (237 milliliters) heavy cream

4 ounces (113 grams) cream cheese, at room temperature

½ cup (125 grams) creamy or chunky peanut butter

2 tablespoons (28 grams) unsalted butter, at room temperature

½ cup (57 grams) powdered sugar

1. In a medium bowl, whip the heavy cream to soft peaks with an electric mixer. Set aside.

2. Combine the cream cheese, peanut butter, and butter in a large bowl and beat with the electric mixer. Sift in the powdered sugar and mix until smooth. Add the whipped cream and mix on low until just combined.

3. Scoop the mousse into the baked and cooled crust and smooth the surface with an offset spatula. The tart crust and filling can be made a day ahead. Store wrapped in the refrigerator until ready to decorate.

2 or 3 green apples, such as Granny Smith

2 or 3 yellow apples, such as Golden Delicious or Opal

Paring knife

1. Cut four sides off each apple, slicing as close to the core as possible but avoiding the seeds. Place the apple sections skin-side up and cut them into ½-inch-wide columns. Rotate 90 degrees and cut the columns every ¼ inch. Each apple rectangle should measure approximately ½ inch by ¼ inch.

2. Starting at the center of the tart, insert a row of green apple pieces in a zigzag herringbone pattern, using the peanut butter mousse to stabilize the apples and hold them in place. Then tightly nestle a row of yellow apple pieces underneath.

3. Continue row by row, alternating colors, until the entire tart surface has been covered.

4. Serve immediately.

SUGGESTED SUBSTITUTIONS

Crust alternatives: Speculoos Cookie Crust (page 29), Chocolate Tart Pastry Shell (page 32)

Topping alternatives: Red apple, pear

NOTE

As a design variation, cut the apples into squares instead of rectangles. Puzzle the apple pieces tightly together in the mousse, randomizing the color order and creating a pixelated visual. Or use a variety of apples across the natural color spectrum (reds, yellows, greens), cut the apples into cubes, and mimic the design process of Berried Treasure (page 89) to create a columnar ombré.

SPIKE A POSE

One of Ben's greatest dreams in life is for us to step out on a casual outing in matching outfits. I cannot fathom anything more mortifying, and while I try my best to be a supportive partner, I do not advocate for this behavior at all. The only exception I allow is our yearly Ko-ristmas card. Every holiday season, we bestow upon our family and friends a themed photo of our wildest concoction. Past ensembles have included vintage ugly Christmas pullovers, form-fitting plaid onesie pajamas complete with functional butt flaps, a two-person Santa sweater, and giant faux fur cheetah print coats. We keep a running list of ideas, and the concepts escalate in absurdity with each passing year.

Since every portrait involves venturing out into public and making complete fools of ourselves, we embrace it unabashedly—power postures and all. This black tea panna cotta, while thoroughly delicious, can come across as a humdrum brown. Draping it in a textured pelt of mango and strawberry reminds me of our Yuletide antics. A dose of sparkle, a bit of pizzazz, a whole lot of brass. Exercise your creative freedom in dressing this tart, and remember, whatever outfit you choose, always strike a pose.

1 fully baked Basic Tart Pastry Shell (page 31), cooled completely

BLACK TEA PANNA COTTA

¾ cup (177 milliliters) heavy cream

2 teaspoons unflavored gelatin

1½ cups (355 milliliters) whole milk

5 black tea bags

3 tablespoons (37 grams) granulated sugar

1. Pour the heavy cream into a small bowl and sprinkle the gelatin evenly over the surface. Let sit for 10 minutes to bloom the gelatin.

2. Meanwhile, gently heat the milk in a small saucepan. Remove from the heat when steam begins to lift off the surface and a tiny line of bubbles forms around the edge. Do not allow it to boil.

3. Steep the tea bags in the milk for 5 minutes, swirling the bags and pressing them with a spatula to extract maximum flavor. Discard the tea bags.

4. Add the sugar to the milk tea, then whisk in the heavy cream and gelatin. Return to low heat, stirring continuously, until the gelatin has dissolved. Strain the mixture through a fine-mesh sieve into a small bowl.

5. Cool the mixture to room temperature, stirring occasionally, then chill in the refrigerator for 30 minutes.

6. Pour the tea mixture into the baked and cooled tart shell and chill until set, about 2 hours, before decorating.

4 to 6 large strawberries

2 small mangos

Chef's knife

Toothpick

1. Hull the strawberries and slice them in half, crown to point. Lay each half cut-side down and slice into ½-inch sections, then cut each section into varying square and triangle pieces.

2. Peel the mangos and cut four sections off the sides of the fruit, slicing as close to the seed as possible. Lay each mango section cut-side down and cut into ½-inch slices. Cut each slice into varying square and triangle pieces, as with the strawberries.

3. Using a toothpick, lightly draw a large zigzag on the surface of the tart, with the points of each zig (and zag) reaching the edge of the tart. Beginning with the left side of the tart, fill the first section by fitting strawberry pieces together, seeded surface up. The differing shapes, heights, and angles of the strawberry pieces will create a textured effect.

4. Fill the next triangle section with mango pieces, fitting the fruit closely together.

5. Continue filling each section with fruit, alternating between strawberries and mangos, until the entire tart surface has been covered.

6. Keep the tart in the refrigerator until serving. This tart is best consumed within 2 days.

SUGGESTED SUBSTITUTIONS

Crust alternative: Matcha Green Tea Tart Pastry Shell (page 35)

Topping alternatives: Blackberry, raspberry

A MARBLE TO BEHOLD

I have a severe phobia of rodents and, for whatever reason, everyone always thinks it's a joke. As if the fear of loathsome mongrels with beady eyes and bald tails who once spread the bubonic plague is merely a punch line.

Once, in the middle of college finals week and in front of an audience, a friend thought it would be amusing to sneak into my apartment and drop his dwarf hamster on me. I panicked, of course, and then, in my sleep-deprived state, proceeded to burst into tears. Big watery drops, blubbering sobs, the whole bit. Mortified, I beat a hasty retreat to the bathroom, but because I was living an episode of *Fear Factor*, the friend-turned-nemesis proceeded to stuff the hamster under the door, trapping me inside with it. I ended up escaping to the dorm of another friend, who wasn't home but whose roommate was getting hot and heavy with her companion on the living room couch. What a time to be alive!

This is the kind of tart you drown your sorrows with, and if I knew anything about pies back then, I would have stress-eaten this entire thing while hiding in someone else's apartment and plotting to burn my own to the ground. With stalwart allies like caramelized onions, creamy potato, and crispy cheese to comfort you, you won't even need friends. Although good ones do sound nice . . .

1 partially baked Herbed Tart Pastry Shell (page 38)

POTATO, ONION, AND PORTER CHEDDAR FILLING

1 large yellow onion

1 tablespoon unsalted butter

½ pound Irish Porter Cheddar cheese

½ pound Yukon gold potatoes (about 2 small waxy potatoes), peeled and cut into ⅛-inch slices

1½ teaspoons kosher salt

¾ cup (177 milliliters) heavy cream

1 egg yolk

1. Cut the onion in half through the root, trim the ends, peel, and cut into ¼-inch half-moon slices.

2. Melt the butter in a large saucepan over medium-high heat. When it begins to sizzle, add half of the onion. Cook until the onion is translucent, about 2 minutes. Add the remaining onion and sauté until softened, about 15 minutes. Turn the heat down to medium-low and cook, stirring frequently and adding a few tablespoons of water if the pan begins to dry out, until the onion is brown and caramelized, 45 to 60 minutes. Spread the caramelized onion in the tart shell. Set aside.

3. Preheat the oven to 350°F.

4. Cut the cheese into ⅛-inch slices. Using a 1-inch rhombus cutter, punch at least 30 shapes out of the cheese, maximizing the number of rhombuses per cheese slice. Finely chop the remaining scraps of cheese and set aside.

5. Place the tart shell on a rimmed baking sheet. Add a single layer of potato slices over the onions and season with

recipe continues

¾ teaspoon of the salt. Sprinkle the chopped scraps of cheese evenly over the potatoes. Layer the remaining potato slices over the cheese and season with the remaining ¾ teaspoon salt.

6. In a small bowl, whisk together the heavy cream and egg yolk. Carefully pour the cream mixture over the tart, letting the liquid sink into the gaps between the potato slices.

MARBLED TILE DESIGN PROCESS

1-inch rhombus cutter (see step 4 above)

30 Irish Porter Cheddar rhombuses

1. Lay a horizontal row of Cheddar rhombuses ⅛ inch apart across the surface of the tart. Place another row below this, inserting rhombuses in the gaps between the shapes in the first row. Cover the tart surface with Cheddar tiles but ensure that there isn't any cheese hanging over the edges.

2. Bake the tart on the rimmed baking sheet for 40 to 45 minutes, until a knife inserted in the center indicates the potatoes are tender. Broil on high for 2 minutes to create a crisp, golden cheese crust.

3. Serve hot with a fresh green salad. Cold slices also make a delicious breakfast the next day . . . if you have any leftovers!

SUGGESTED SUBSTITUTIONS

Crust alternative: Everything (but the) Bagel Tart Pastry Shell (page 36)

Topping alternatives: Any Cheddar will work, although you'll miss out on the beautiful marbling effect of the Porter Cheddar.

NOTE

I'll be honest here . . . the precise tiling of this design bakes out (but is replaced by a magical marbling effect!). Perhaps you've had a rough day and need the release that comes with the meditative process of cutting cheese (there was bound to be at least one fart-adjacent joke in this book!). In this case, follow the recipe as directed and relish your Instagramable pre-bake shot. If it's been one of *those* days and you can't be bothered with intricate shapes, simple slices of cheese will result in the a crispy, marbled cheese crust all the same. Your call, but you know what I'd choose . . . tart (fart) art.

PIEOMETRY

THE FIG IS UP

One evening, after a hefty family meal, I asked my mom if I could have a piece of chocolate. She responded with, "Let's take a breather first." So naturally, my small-year-old self took a huuuuge inhale, huffed it out in a hurry, and declared myself officially ready for chocolate.

Ironically, I choked on a Hershey's Kiss several years later because I accidentally inhaled when I popped it into my mouth. I've had a bittersweet relationship with chocolate ever since, but this is one of the simpler tarts in the book to execute, so I still reach for the recipe regularly. In the time it takes to complete a breathing exercise, you'll have a glossy ganache ready to appease the demands of the hesitant and enthusiastic alike.

1 fully baked Chocolate Tart Pastry Shell (page 32), cooled completely

CHOCOLATE HAZELNUT GANACHE

¾ cup (130 grams) shelled hazelnuts

8 ounces (227 grams) bittersweet chocolate, finely chopped

2 tablespoons (28 grams) unsalted butter, at room temperature, cut into ½-inch cubes

1 cup (237 milliliters) heavy cream

1. Preheat the oven to 350°F.

2. Spread the hazelnuts in a single layer on a rimmed baking sheet. Toast for 10 to 12 minutes, until the nuts are golden brown. Place the nuts in a clean kitchen towel and rub off the skins. Roughly chop the roasted hazelnuts and sprinkle them evenly in the tart shell. Set aside.

3. Combine the chocolate, butter, and heavy cream in a heatproof bowl and set the bowl over a double boiler. Melt the chocolate and butter in the cream, gently stirring occasionally. Remove from the heat as soon as the ganache is completely smooth.

4. Pour the ganache into the baked and cooled tart shell over the hazelnuts. Smooth the surface with an offset spatula, popping any bubbles with a toothpick. Let cool on the counter before decorating.

FIG TILE DESIGN PROCESS

4 large figs

Paring knife

Toothpick

Ruler

1. Lay a ruler vertically down the center of the tart, resting it on the edges of the pan. Following the ruler edge, lightly trace a line down the center of the tart with a toothpick or the tip of your knife. Draw two additional lines on either side of the center divider, each spaced 2 inches from the center line, then two more short lines 2 inches to the other side of those new lines. You will have five vertical lines on the surface of your tart.

2. Trim the figs and cut them into ¼-inch crosswise slices. Cut each fig slice into quarters.

3. Starting at the top of the center line, place a fig quarter with one straight side on the line. Configure the round edge to face northwest. Next, place another fig quarter below, its rounded edge facing southeast and a straight side on the line. The rounded edge of the next quarter should face southwest, and the fourth quarter should face northeast. Continue placing fig quarters down the line in this rotation, and repeat the same process with the other lines.

4. Let stand at room temperature for 1 to 2 hours to set before serving. This tart is best consumed within 2 days.

SUGGESTED SUBSTITUTIONS

Crust alternatives: Basic Tart Pastry Shell (page 31), Matcha Green Tea Tart Pastry Shell (page 35)

Topping alternatives: Kumquat, orange, cantaloupe, kiwi

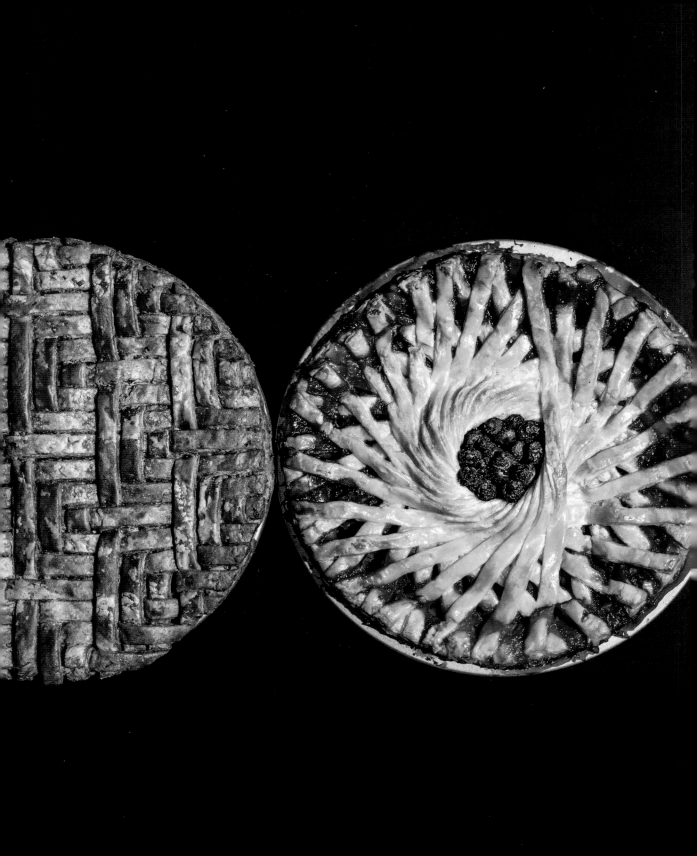

PIE PRIMER

PIE-D AND TRUE

I wish I had kept a tally of every pie I've made since that very first one in 2016. But as I never expected pie to become such a *thing* in my life, I simply have to guestimate that I've made over a thousand in my home kitchen since then. When you do anything that many times, you naturally acquire a few tips and tricks along the way. Here are some you may find useful in your own pie-jinks.

MAKING DOUGH: Pie dough maintains a reputation as finicky and difficult, but with these recipes and some repetition, anyone can master a flaky crust.

Keep your ingredients cold and, whenever possible, your environment, too. Be assertive (dough can sense fear), but don't be overinvolved. Unlike bread-making, pie dough does not require any kneading and, in fact, overworking the dough with too much touching can lead to a tough crust.

Use your instincts. If the recipe calls for 4 tablespoons water but the dough is still feeling dry and crumbly, add a bit more liquid. Crust yourself, and with some confidence and practice, you'll be well on your way to flying pie.

If you're just starting out on your pie journey and want to assess the quality of your dough before getting too far in the process, cut the dough disk in half (before the resting period) and check for stacks of striated layers. These foreshadow a future baked crust full of gorgeous flakes! Then gently press the halves back together, wrap in plastic, and rest before rolling as directed.

COLORING DOUGH: This book includes an array of formulas for making colored pie dough in basic colors, but experimenting with different juices and powders to achieve more sophisticated hues is highly encouraged. Keep proportions in mind, though, as dough only requires so much liquid and add-

ing significantly more powder will deepen the color but also affect the final texture of the crust.

ROLLING DOUGH: I roll out my pie dough directly on the counter, so flouring the surface and my rolling pin before and during the rolling process is crucial. I continuously rotate my dough 45 degrees as I roll to ensure it isn't sticking to the counter, and when I have achieved the desired size I transfer the dough to parchment. If you're rolling and the dough isn't moving outward, it's probably stuck to your work surface. Gently pull or scrape it up, flour the surface, and resume. Alternatively, you can roll dough directly on parchment paper or a pastry cloth made of cotton canvas.

Rotating the dough 45 or 90 degrees every few rolls can also help with achieving even circles and rectangles. Consistently obtaining nicely shaped rolled dough largely comes with repetition and practice, though, so don't stress too much if you're a beginner and find yourself rolling cumulus clouds or other gorgeous blobs instead.

CUTTING STRIPS: Always make sure your rolled-out dough is on a sheet of parchment before you cut strips. If they end up in an inconvenient spot on your counter or start to get warm and mushy, it's nearly impossible to move them without marring the strips' crisp lines. With parchment, it's easy to slide a baking sheet underneath to stick in the fridge at a moment's notice.

If you are right-handed like me, you'll find it easiest to start from the right side of the rectangle and work your way left. I also prefer to run my pastry wheel bottom to top, but find the rhythm that works best for you.

When you're using a ruler to align topping elements or to draw a line with a toothpick, use slight pressure (but not so much as to leave indentations in the dough) to hold it in place. I usually outstretch my left hand so my middle finger secures the top of the ruler and the bottom with my thumb. This prevents the ruler from sliding around and ensures straight and even strips.

I never measure the width of each individual strip because I only possess so much insanity (contrary to popular belief). Eyeballing and approximating each strip is the path of least resistance and will save time, but uniformity plays a key role in the visual impact of your final design, so try to make them as even and consistent as possible.

FREEZING PIES AND DOUGH: Wrapped and rested disks of pie dough can be sealed in a bag or container and frozen for up to 4 months. Let the dough thaw in the refrigerator overnight before rolling.

If you are freezing a complete pie to bake at a later date, place the pie on a level surface in the freezer for 1 hour to set the design completely, then wrap tightly in several layers of plastic and label with the flavor and date. Do not thaw the pie before baking, and add 30 to 45 minutes to the total baking time. (A handful of pies in this book are not suitable for freezing. Notes have been included in the recipes for these specific cases.)

BAKING PIES

EGG WASHING: For pies that utilize the Basic or Whole Wheat Cheddar Chive dough, an egg wash can add an extra dimension of deep golden shine that is hard to resist. Note: I rarely egg wash colored doughs to preserve the vibrancy of the color.

> Milk: brown matte finish
> Egg white: clear and shiny finish
> One whole egg: yellow and shiny finish
> One whole egg with a splash of heavy cream: deep golden shiny finish

BLIND BAKING: Some pie fillings (like Curls of Wisdom on page 170 and Once in a Tile on page 173) require a shorter bake time than it takes to fully bake the crust. Blind baking ensures the dough is cooked through and crisp while not overcooking your filling. Freeze your pie dough solid in the tin, line tightly with foil, and fill up the sides with pie weights for best results.

BAKING TEMPERATURE: I always bake pies at a higher heat for the first 20 to 25 minutes to help set the design. Then I turn the heat down to allow the filling to cook through without scorching the crust. If the crust edges are browning rapidly, cover with a shield. If the entire pie top is browning too quickly, lightly rest a sheet of foil on the surface and remove for the last 5 to 10 minutes of baking to allow the crust to cook through.

The vibrancy of the colored pie doughs will fade a bit during the baking process. I like to bake at lower heat (as compared to pies with plain dough where deep golden is the goal) to help preserve the color. The higher the heat and the longer you bake the pie, the more the color will fade. If you find the color of your dough diminishing early on in its bake, resting a sheet of foil over the top of the pie can help staunch the fade.

BAKING TIME FOR FRUIT PIES: Baking pies with fresh fruit can be occasionally unpredictable. You may have a batch of berries or cherries that are particularly juicy, especially crops at peak season. The filling recipes in this book don't call for maceration (tossing the fruit in sugar to release its juices) and then reduction of those juices since it adds an extra few steps to an often already long process, so the total baking time can be variable. I've provided recommended time ranges here to serve as a guide, but do supplement with following your instincts. If you've reached the high end of the timing range and the filling isn't yet bubbling through the center or the dough still looks undercooked, keep baking!

CUTTING BAKED PIES: Exercise supreme self-control and allow pies to cool completely before cutting to achieve cleaner slices. Some pie fillings are juicier than others, but if you cut into a pie while still hot, it will be soup!

PIE CRACKERS AND PIE COOKIES: Surplus dough scraps can also be gently pressed into a ball (do not knead), wrapped tightly in plastic, and chilled before re-rolling once as marbled dough (page 160). Or (bonus snack

#YEAHBUTWHATDOESITLOOKLIKEBAKED: I first got into pie design primarily motivated by the art of it, so initially, I only showcased pies in all their pristine pre-bake glory. Yes, ultimately all the pies I make get baked, and *of course* baking alters the final product. If I sat in a 400°F oven for 90 minutes, I'd certainly come out changed. Still, I feel that the transformation of an art piece does not detract from its aesthetic value at any point of its process, so the crisp precision and sharp colors of the design before it goes in the oven can still be appreciated. Even if the lines become blurred and the colors more muted.

I quickly learned that people have a lot of feelings about this. While the response to Lokokitchen has largely been positive, I've also received numerous vitriolic messages, emails, and in-person lectures invalidating my work and denouncing me as a fraud because of the pre-bake/baked debate. Pieometry critics also decry the effort that goes into crafting designs that ultimately mutate as a complete waste of time.

To these ends, I recommend having a glass of wine and channeling that energy into other issues of greater import. If you've ever wondered about the #yeahbutwhatdoesitlooklikebaked hashtag, that was my other response. But mainly, I have this to say: I make these pies because I enjoy the process. It's soothing and meditative and creative and fun, and it's a way for me to combine my love of art, baking, and feeding those around me into one marvelous pastime. I hope that whatever you get out of it—because sometimes it's about the destination and sometimes it's the journey—also brings you joy.

incentive alert!), the scraps can be placed on a baking sheet lined with parchment paper and baked at 350°F until cooked through and crisp, 10 to 20 minutes depending on the size and thickness of the scraps. There is plenty of flexibility for customization here. The scraps can be egg washed and sprinkled with demerara sugar for crunch. They can be baked bare and tossed hot in cinnamon sugar right out of the oven. They can even be egg washed and sprinkled with freshly grated Parmesan cheese and herbs as savory morsels!

PIE DOUGHS

BASIC PIE DOUGH

WHITE

This is the foundational piece for making all your pie dreams come alive. Master this dough and you master them all. While the ingredient quantities may differ slightly for the naturally colored dough variations, the process remains the same. Dry ingredients get tossed together, the butter jumps in next, and then the liquid is added as the last step. Follow this formula for both the manual and food processor methods across the spectrum of colors.

Pay careful attention to the number of dough disks called for in each design recipe. In the case where multiple disks of the same type of dough are required, I recommend doubling the recipe and making two disks at a time. In fact, since freezing pie dough is so easy and effective, I often make two disks at a time even when I'm making a single-crust pie, saving the spare for an expedited future baking session.

½ cup ice

½ cup (118 milliliters) cold water

1¼ cups (175 grams) all-purpose flour

½ tablespoon granulated sugar

½ teaspoon kosher salt

½ cup (1 stick/113 grams) cold unsalted butter, cut into ½-inch cubes

MANUAL METHOD

1. Combine the ice and water in a small cup or bowl. Set aside.

2. Put the flour, sugar, and salt in a large bowl and stir with a spatula to combine.

3. Sprinkle in the butter cubes and toss until each cube is coated in the flour mixture.

4. Flatten each cube of butter with your pointer fingers and thumbs. Toss again to coat the flattened butter pieces. Continue massaging the butter into the flour until the remaining shards resemble cornflakes in a range of sizes.

5. Add 2 tablespoons of the cold water, taking care not to include any ice, and fluff the moisture through the flour with a spatula. Continue adding cold water 1 tablespoon at a time, pressing the dough with a spatula after each addition until it begins to come together. Avoid any heavy kneading, as overworking the dough will lead to a tough crust.

6. If the dough still has quite a bit of dry mix and doesn't hold together when a handful is squeezed, add a little more water. Be careful not to add too much water (usually 3 to 5 tablespoons total are sufficient). The dough should be smooth and supple. If the dough is quite tacky, you've likely

added too much liquid. Try gently incorporating a little more flour. If it is still very sticky, I suggest starting over with a new batch of ingredients. Overly hydrated dough will be difficult to roll out and utilize in these designs, and the crust will likely be tough when baked. Pie fries or pie cookies (see page 130) may be a suitable option for keeping the handling to a minimum and avoiding outright waste of the dough.

recipe continues

7. When the dough begins to hold together, turn it out onto your work surface and gently form it into a rounded mound with your hands. Wrap the dough tightly in plastic, then gently press it into a round, flat disk, about 5 inches in diameter and 1 inch in thickness. Refrigerate for at least 3 hours or overnight before rolling. Resting the dough in the fridge allows the gluten to relax and the dough to fully hydrate, and prevents shrinkage during baking. If you plan to freeze the pie dough, do so only after the rest period of at least 3 hours in the fridge.

8. Use the dough in the recipe of your choice.

FOOD PROCESSOR METHOD

1. Combine the ice and water in a small cup or bowl. Set aside.

2. Put the flour, sugar, and salt in a food processor and pulse several times to incorporate. Sprinkle the butter cubes evenly over the surface of the dry mixture and pulse quickly 20 to 25 times to break up the cubes into small jaggedy pieces.

3. Turn the mixture out into a large mixing bowl. Sift through with a spatula for unprocessed butter cubes and flatten any pieces larger than a pecan half with your pointer finger and thumb.

4. Add 2 tablespoons of the cold water, taking care not to include any ice, and stir through with a spatula. Continue adding water 1 tablespoon at a time, pressing the dough with your hands or a spatula after each addition until it begins to come together. Avoid any heavy kneading, as overworking the dough will lead to a tough crust.

5. If the dough still has quite a bit of dry mix and doesn't hold together when a handful is squeezed, add a little more water. Be careful not to add too much water (usually 3 to 5 tablespoons total are sufficient). The dough should be smooth and supple.

6. When the dough begins to hold together, turn it out onto your work surface and gently form it into a mound with your hands. Wrap the dough tightly in plastic, then gently press it into a round, flat disk, about 5 inches in diameter and 1 inch in thickness. Refrigerate for at least 3 hours or overnight before rolling. Resting the dough in the fridge allows the gluten to relax and the dough to fully hydrate, and prevents shrinkage during baking. If you plan to freeze the pie dough, do so only after the rest period of at least 3 hours in the fridge.

7. Use the dough in the recipe of your choice.

BEET PIE DOUGH

MAGENTA

MAKES 1 DISK OF PIE DOUGH, TO MAKE A SINGLE-CRUST PIE

The beet powder is optional in this recipe but is incredibly effective at creating a deep, bake-resilient magenta-colored dough.

1¼ cups (175 grams) all-purpose flour

½ tablespoon granulated sugar

½ teaspoon kosher salt

1 tablespoon beet powder (see page 16; optional)

½ cup (1 stick/113 grams) cold unsalted butter, cut into ½-inch cubes

½ cup (118 milliliters) cold beet juice (see page 140)

MANUAL METHOD

1. Keep the beet juice in the refrigerator until step 5.

2. Put the flour, sugar, salt, and beet powder, if using, in a large bowl and stir with a spatula to combine.

3. Sprinkle in the butter cubes and toss until each cube is coated in the flour mixture.

4. Flatten each cube of butter with your pointer fingers and thumbs. Toss again to coat the flattened butter pieces. Continue massaging the butter into the flour until the remaining shards resemble cornflakes in a range of sizes.

5. Remove the beet juice from the refrigerator. Add 2 tablespoons of the juice and fluff the moisture through the flour with a spatula. Continue adding juice 1 tablespoon at a time, pressing the dough with a spatula after each addition until it begins to come together. Avoid any heavy kneading, as overworking the dough will lead to a tough crust.

6. If the dough still has quite a bit of dry mix and doesn't hold together when a handful is squeezed, add a little more juice. Be careful not to add too much liquid (usually 3 to 5 tablespoons total are sufficient). The dough should be smooth and supple. If the dough is quite tacky, you've likely added too much liquid. Try gently incorporating a little more flour. If it is still very sticky, I suggest starting over with a new batch of ingredients. Overly hydrated dough will be difficult to roll out and utilize in these designs, and the crust will likely be tough when baked. Pie fries or pie cookies (see page 130) may be a suitable option for keeping the handling to a minimum and avoiding outright waste of the dough.

7. When the dough begins to hold together, turn it out onto your work surface and gently form it into a rounded mound with your hands. Wrap the dough tightly in plastic, then gently press it into a round, flat disk, about 5 inches in diameter and 1 inch in thickness. Refrigerate for at least 3 hours or overnight before rolling. Resting the dough in the fridge allows the gluten to relax and the dough to fully hydrate, and prevents shrinkage during baking. If you plan to freeze the pie dough, do so only after the rest period of at least 3 hours in the fridge.

8. Use the dough in the recipe of your choice.

FOOD PROCESSOR METHOD

1. Keep the beet juice in the refrigerator until step 4.

2. Put the flour, sugar, salt, and beet powder, if using, in a food processor and pulse several times to incorporate. Sprinkle the butter cubes evenly over the surface of the dry mixture and pulse quickly 20 to 25 times to break up the cubes into smaller jaggedy pieces.

3. Turn the mixture out into a large mixing bowl. Sift through with a spatula for unprocessed butter cubes and flatten any pieces larger than a pecan half with your pointer finger and thumb.

4. Remove the beet juice from the refrigerator. Add 2 tablespoons of the juice and stir through with a spatula. Continue adding juice 1 tablespoon at a time, pressing the dough with your hands or a spatula after each addition until it begins to come together. Avoid any heavy kneading, as overworking the dough will lead to a tough crust.

5. If the dough still has quite a bit of dry mix and doesn't hold together when a handful is squeezed, add a little more juice. Be careful not to add too much liquid (usually 3 to 5 tablespoons total are sufficient). The dough should be smooth and supple. If the dough is quite tacky, you've likely added too much liquid. Try gently incorporating a little more flour. If it is still very sticky, I suggest starting over with a new batch of ingredients. Overly hydrated dough will be difficult to roll out and utilize in these designs, and the crust will likely be

recipe continues

tough when baked. Pie fries or pie cookies (see page 130) may be a suitable option for keeping the handling to a minimum and avoiding outright waste of the dough.

6. When the dough begins to hold together, turn it out onto your work surface and gently form it into a mound with your hands. Wrap the dough tightly in plastic, then gently press it into a round, flat disk, about 5 inches in diameter and 1 inch in thickness. Refrigerate for at least 3 hours or overnight before rolling. Resting the dough in the fridge allows the gluten to relax and the dough to fully hydrate, and prevents shrinkage during baking. If you plan to freeze the pie dough, do so only after the rest period of at least 3 hours in the fridge.

7. Use the dough in the recipe of your choice.

BEET JUICE

The manual method for extracting beet liquid doesn't result in juice, per se, but the liquid by-product is so vibrantly colored, it still works well for coloring pie dough. The depth of the coloring may be variable kitchen to kitchen, but if you're concerned the liquid is too light, the addition of beet powder can serve to further intensify the color.

MANUAL METHOD (MAKES ABOUT 1 CUP)

1 pound red beets, trimmed, peeled, and roughly chopped

2 cups water

1. Combine the beet chunks and water in a small saucepan and bring to a boil. Cook until the beets are fork-tender and the remaining liquid is a deep burgundy color. Chill the beets and cooking liquid in the refrigerator until cold.

2. Strain out the beets and reserve for another use. Keep the cooking liquid refrigerated until you use it.

ELECTRIC JUICER METHOD (MAKES ABOUT 1 CUP)

1½ pounds (680 grams) red beets, trimmed, peeled, and roughly chopped

1. Run the beet chunks through an electric juicer. Discard the remaining pulp and pass the juice through a fine-mesh sieve twice. Skim off any residual foam.

2. Refrigerate the juice until cold before using.

BLACK SESAME PIE DOUGH
WHITE AND BLACK SPECKLE

MAKES 1 DISK OF PIE DOUGH, TO MAKE A SINGLE-CRUST PIE

In this dough, the apple cider vinegar lends a touch of acidity that contrasts nicely with the nutty sesame seeds.

½ cup ice

½ cup (118 milliliters) cold water

1 tablespoon apple cider vinegar

1¼ cups (175 grams) all-purpose flour

2 tablespoons black sesame seeds (see page 17)

½ tablespoon granulated sugar

½ teaspoon kosher salt

½ cup (1 stick/113 grams) cold unsalted butter, cut into ½-inch cubes

MANUAL METHOD

1. Combine the ice, water, and apple cider vinegar in a small cup or bowl. Set aside.

2. Put the flour, sesame seeds, sugar, and salt in a large bowl and stir with a spatula to combine.

3. Sprinkle in the butter cubes and toss until each cube is coated in the flour mixture.

4. Flatten each cube of butter with your pointer fingers and thumbs. Toss again to coat the flattened butter pieces. Continue massaging the butter into the flour until the remaining shards resemble cornflakes in a range of sizes.

5. Add 2 tablespoons of the cold vinegar-water mixture, taking care not to include any ice, and fluff the moisture through the flour with a spatula. Continue adding liquid 1 tablespoon at a time, pressing the dough with a spatula after each addition until it begins to come together. Avoid any heavy kneading, as overworking the dough will lead to a tough crust.

6. If the dough still has quite a bit of dry mix and doesn't hold together when a handful is squeezed, add a little more liquid. Be careful not to add too much water (usually 3 to 5 tablespoons total are sufficient). The dough should be smooth and supple. If the dough is quite tacky, you've likely added too much liquid. Try gently incorporating a little more flour. If it is still very sticky, I suggest starting over with a new batch of ingredients. Overly hydrated dough will be difficult to roll out and utilize in these designs, and the crust will likely be tough when baked. Pie fries or pie cookies (see page 130) may be a suitable option for keeping the handling to a minimum and avoiding outright waste of the dough.

recipe continues

PIE DOUGHS

7. When the dough begins to hold together, turn it out onto your work surface and gently form it into a rounded mound with your hands. Wrap the dough tightly in plastic, then gently press it into a round, flat disk, about 5 inches in diameter and 1 inch in thickness. Refrigerate for at least 3 hours or overnight before rolling. Resting the dough in the fridge allows the gluten to relax and the dough to fully hydrate, and prevents shrinkage during baking. If you plan to freeze the pie dough, do so only after the rest period of at least 3 hours in the fridge.

8. Use the dough in the recipe of your choice.

FOOD PROCESSOR METHOD

1. Combine the ice, water, and apple cider vinegar in a small cup or bowl. Set aside.

2. Put the flour, sesame seeds, sugar, and salt in a food processor and pulse several times to incorporate. Sprinkle the butter cubes evenly over the surface of the dry mixture and pulse quickly 20 to 25 times to break up the cubes into smaller jaggedy pieces.

3. Turn the mixture out into a large mixing bowl. Sift through with a spatula for unprocessed butter cubes and flatten any pieces larger than a pecan half with your pointer finger and thumb.

4. Add 2 tablespoons of the cold vinegar-water mixture, taking care not to include any ice, and stir through with a spatula. Continue adding liquid 1 tablespoon at a time, pressing the dough with your hands or a spatula after each addition until it begins to come together. Avoid any heavy kneading, as overworking the dough will lead to a tough crust.

5. If the dough still has quite a bit of dry mix and doesn't hold together when a handful is squeezed, add a little more liquid. Be careful not to add too much water (usually 3 to 5 tablespoons total are sufficient). The dough should be smooth and supple. If the dough is quite tacky, you've likely added too much liquid. Try gently incorporating a little more flour. If it is still very sticky, I suggest starting over with a new batch of ingredients. Overly hydrated dough will be difficult to roll out and utilize in these designs, and the crust will likely be

tough when baked. Pie fries or pie cookies (see page 130) may be a suitable option for keeping the handling to a minimum and avoiding outright waste of the dough.

6. When the dough begins to hold together, turn it out onto your work surface and gently form it into a mound with your hands. Wrap the dough tightly in plastic, then gently press it into a round, flat disk, about 5 inches in diameter and 1 inch in thickness. Refrigerate for at least 3 hours or overnight before rolling. Resting the dough in the fridge allows the gluten to relax and the dough to fully hydrate, and prevents shrinkage during baking. If you plan to freeze the pie dough, do so only after the rest period of at least 3 hours in the fridge.

7. Use the dough in the recipe of your choice.

BLUEBERRY PIE DOUGH
DARK PURPLE

MAKES 1 DISK OF PIE DOUGH, TO MAKE A SINGLE-CRUST PIE

In this recipe, the blueberry powder is not optional, as the juice alone does not tint the dough a dark enough shade to hold through baking.

1¼ cups (175 grams) all-purpose flour

½ tablespoon granulated sugar

½ teaspoon kosher salt

3 tablespoons (30 grams) blueberry powder (see page 16)

½ cup (1 stick/113 grams) cold unsalted butter, cut into ½-inch cubes

½ cup (118 milliliters) cold pure blueberry juice

Every attempt at producing blueberry juice on my own has resulted in a sludgy mix that oxidized and turned brown almost immediately. Instead, I rely on Bow Hill Blueberries or Lakewood Organic for their cold-pressed 100 percent blueberry juices. Anything with added ingredients and sugar won't produce the same results.

MANUAL METHOD

1. Keep the blueberry juice in the refrigerator until step 5.

2. Put the flour, sugar, salt, and blueberry powder in a large bowl and stir with a spatula to combine.

3. Sprinkle in the butter cubes and toss until each cube is coated in the flour mixture.

4. Flatten each cube of butter with your pointer fingers and thumbs. Toss again to coat the flattened butter pieces. Continue massaging the butter into the flour until the remaining shards resemble cornflakes in a range of sizes.

5. Remove the blueberry juice from the refrigerator. Add 2 tablespoons of the juice and fluff the moisture through the flour with a spatula. Continue adding juice 1 tablespoon at a time, pressing the dough with a spatula after each addition until it begins to come together. Avoid any heavy kneading, as overworking the dough will lead to a tough crust.

6. If the dough still has quite a bit of dry mix and doesn't hold together when a handful is squeezed, add a little more juice. Be careful not to add too much liquid (usually 3 to 5 tablespoons total are sufficient). The dough should be smooth and supple. If the dough is quite tacky, you've likely added too much liquid. Try gently incorporating a little more flour. If it is still very sticky, I suggest starting over with a new

batch of ingredients. Overly hydrated dough will be difficult to roll out and utilize in these designs, and the crust will likely be tough when baked. Pie fries or pie cookies (see page 130) may be a suitable option for keeping the handling to a minimum and avoiding outright waste of the dough.

7. When the dough begins to hold together, turn it out onto your work surface and gently form it into a rounded mound with your hands. Wrap the dough tightly in plastic, then gently press it into a round, flat disk, about 5 inches in diameter and 1 inch in thickness. Refrigerate for at least 3 hours or overnight before rolling. Resting the dough in the fridge allows the gluten to relax and the dough to fully hydrate, and prevents shrinkage during baking. If you plan to freeze the pie dough, do so only after the rest period of at least 3 hours in the fridge.

8. Use the dough in the recipe of your choice.

FOOD PROCESSOR METHOD

1. Keep the blueberry juice in the refrigerator until step 4.

2. Put the flour, sugar, salt, and blueberry powder in a food processor and pulse several times to incorporate. Sprinkle the butter cubes evenly over the surface of the dry mixture and pulse quickly 20 to 25 times to break up the cubes into smaller jaggedy pieces.

3. Turn the mixture out into a large mixing bowl. Sift through with a spatula for unprocessed butter cubes and flatten any pieces larger than a pecan half with your pointer finger and thumb.

4. Remove the blueberry juice from the refrigerator. Add 2 tablespoons of the juice and stir through with a spatula. Continue adding juice 1 tablespoon at a time, pressing the dough with your hands or a spatula after each addition until it begins to come together. Avoid any heavy kneading, as overworking the dough will lead to a tough crust.

5. If the dough still has quite a bit of dry mix and doesn't hold together when a handful is squeezed, add a little more juice. Be careful not to add too much liquid (usually 3 to 5 tablespoons total are sufficient). The dough should be

recipe continues

PIE DOUGHS

smooth and supple. If the dough is quite tacky, you've likely added too much liquid. Try gently incorporating a little more flour. If it is still very sticky, I suggest starting over with a new batch of ingredients. Overly hydrated dough will be difficult to roll out and utilize in these designs, and the crust will likely be tough when baked. Pie fries or pie cookies (see page 130) may be a suitable option for keeping the handling to a minimum and avoiding outright waste of the dough.

6. When the dough begins to hold together, turn it out onto your work surface and gently form it into a mound with your hands. Wrap the dough tightly in plastic, then gently press it into a round, flat disk, about 5 inches in diameter and 1 inch in thickness. Refrigerate for at least 3 hours or overnight before rolling. Resting the dough in the fridge allows the gluten to relax and the dough to fully hydrate, and prevents shrinkage during baking. If you plan to freeze the pie dough, do so only after the rest period of at least 3 hours in the fridge.

7. Use the dough in the recipe of your choice.

BUTTERFLY PEA FLOWER PIE DOUGH
DENIM-WASH BLUE

MAKES 1 DISK OF PIE DOUGH, TO MAKE A SINGLE-CRUST PIE

The butterfly pea flower powder is optional in this recipe but is incredibly effective at creating a deep, bake-resilient blue-colored dough.

1¼ cups (175 grams) all-purpose flour

½ tablespoon granulated sugar

½ teaspoon kosher salt

½ tablespoon butterfly pea flower powder (see page 16; optional)

½ cup (1 stick/113 grams) cold unsalted butter, cut into ½-inch cubes

½ cup (118 milliliters) cold butterfly pea flower tea (see page 149)

Butterfly pea flowers are a blossom from southeast Asia. I source my food-grade dried butterfly pea flowers online.

MANUAL METHOD

1. Keep the strained butterfly pea flower tea in the refrigerator until step 5.

2. Put the flour, sugar, salt, and butterfly pea flower powder, if using, in a large bowl and stir with a spatula to combine.

3. Sprinkle in the butter cubes and toss until each cube is coated in the flour mixture.

4. Flatten each cube of butter with your pointer fingers and thumbs. Toss again to coat the flattened butter pieces. Continue massaging the butter into the flour until the remaining shards resemble cornflakes in a range of sizes.

5. Remove the butterfly pea flower tea from the refrigerator. Add 2 tablespoons of the tea and fluff the moisture through the flour with a spatula. Continue adding tea 1 tablespoon at a time, pressing the dough with a spatula after each addition until it begins to come together. Avoid any heavy kneading, as overworking the dough will lead to a tough crust.

6. If the dough still has quite a bit of dry mix and doesn't hold together when a handful is squeezed, add a little more tea. Be careful not to add too much liquid (usually 3 to 5 tablespoons total are sufficient). The dough should be smooth and supple. If the dough is quite tacky, you've likely added too much liquid. Try gently incorporating a little more flour. If it is still very sticky, I suggest starting over with a new batch of ingredients.

recipe continues

Overly hydrated dough will be difficult to roll out and utilize in these designs, and the crust will likely be tough when baked. Pie fries or pie cookies (see page 130) may be a suitable option for keeping the handling to a minimum and avoiding outright waste of the dough.

7. When the dough begins to hold together, turn it out onto your work surface and gently form it into a rounded mound with your hands. Wrap the dough tightly in plastic, then gently press it into a round, flat disk, about 5 inches in diameter and 1 inch in thickness. Refrigerate for at least 3 hours or overnight before rolling. Resting the dough in the fridge allows the gluten to relax and the dough to fully hydrate, and prevents shrinkage during baking. If you plan to freeze the pie dough, do so only after the rest period of at least 3 hours in the fridge.

8. Use the dough in the recipe of your choice.

FOOD PROCESSOR METHOD

1. Keep the strained butterfly pea flower tea in the refrigerator until step 4.

2. Put the flour, sugar, salt, and butterfly pea flower powder, if using, in a food processor and pulse several times to incorporate. Sprinkle the butter cubes evenly over the surface of the dry mixture and pulse quickly 20 to 25 times to break up the cubes into smaller jaggedy pieces.

3. Turn the mixture out into a large mixing bowl. Sift through with a spatula for unprocessed butter cubes and flatten any pieces larger than a pecan half with your pointer finger and thumb.

4. Remove the butterfly pea flower tea from the refrigerator. Add 2 tablespoons of the tea and stir through with a spatula. Continue adding tea 1 tablespoon at a time, pressing the dough with your hands or a spatula after each addition until it begins to come together. Avoid any heavy kneading, as overworking the dough will lead to a tough crust.

5. If the dough still has quite a bit of dry mix and doesn't hold together when a handful is squeezed, add a little more tea. Be careful not to add too much liquid (usually 3 to 5 tablespoons total are sufficient). The dough should be smooth and supple.

If the dough is quite tacky, you've likely added too much liquid. Try gently incorporating a little more flour. If it is still very sticky, I suggest starting over with a new batch of ingredients. Overly hydrated dough will be difficult to roll out and utilize in these designs, and the crust will likely be tough when baked. Pie fries or pie cookies (see page 130) may be a suitable option for keeping the handling to a minimum and avoiding outright waste of the dough.

6. When the dough begins to hold together, turn it out onto your work surface and gently form it into a mound with your hands. Wrap the dough tightly in plastic, then gently press it into a round, flat disk, about 5 inches in diameter and 1 inch in thickness. Refrigerate for at least 3 hours or overnight before rolling. Resting the dough in the fridge allows the gluten to relax and the dough to fully hydrate, and prevents shrinkage during baking. If you plan to freeze the pie dough, do so only after the rest period of at least 3 hours in the fridge.

7. Use the dough in the recipe of your choice.

BUTTERFLY PEA FLOWER TEA

MAKES 1 CUP (237 MILLILITERS), ENOUGH TO MAKE 2 DOUGH DISKS

⅓ cup (0.25 ounce) dried butterfly pea flowers (see page 14)

1 cup boiling hot water

1. Steep the butterfly pea flowers in the hot water, stirring occasionally.

2. When the water has reached room temperature, place the liquid in the refrigerator to continue steeping overnight.

3. Before using, strain the tea through a fine-mesh sieve, using a spatula to extract as much liquid from the flowers as possible. Discard the flowers or save to steep again. If reusing steeped flowers, the tea will be less vibrant with subsequent batches and the color may not hold in a baked pie.

CARROT PIE DOUGH

ORANGE

MAKES 1 DISK OF PIE DOUGH, TO MAKE A SINGLE-CRUST PIE

The carrot powder is optional in this recipe but is great for creating a more vibrant, bake-resilient orange-colored dough.

1¼ cups (175 grams) all-purpose flour

½ tablespoon granulated sugar

½ teaspoon kosher salt

½ tablespoon carrot powder (see page 16; optional)

½ cup (1 stick/113 grams) cold unsalted butter, cut into ½-inch cubes

½ cup (118 milliliters) cold fresh carrot juice

MANUAL METHOD

1. Keep the carrot juice in the refrigerator until step 5.

2. Put the flour, sugar, salt, and carrot powder, if using, in a large bowl and stir with a spatula to combine.

3. Sprinkle in the butter cubes and toss until each cube is coated in the flour mixture.

4. Flatten each cube of butter with your pointer fingers and thumbs. Toss again to coat the flattened butter pieces. Continue massaging the butter into the flour until the remaining shards resemble cornflakes in a range of sizes.

5. Remove the carrot juice from the refrigerator. Add 2 tablespoons of the juice and fluff the moisture through the flour with a spatula. Continue adding juice 1 tablespoon at a time, pressing the dough with a spatula after each addition until it begins to come together. Avoid any heavy kneading, as overworking the dough will lead to a tough crust.

6. If the dough still has quite a bit of dry mix and doesn't hold together when a handful is squeezed, add a little more juice. Be careful not to add too much liquid (usually 3 to 5 tablespoons total are sufficient). The dough should be smooth and supple. If the dough is quite tacky, you've likely added too much liquid. Try gently incorporating a little more flour. If it is still very sticky, I suggest starting over with a new batch of ingredients. Overly hydrated dough will be difficult to roll out and utilize in these designs, and the crust will likely be tough when baked. Pie fries or pie cookies (see page 130) may be a suitable option for keeping the handling to a minimum and avoiding outright waste of the dough.

7. When the dough begins to hold together, turn it out onto your work surface and gently form it into a rounded mound with your hands. Wrap the dough tightly in plastic, then gently press it into a round, flat disk, about 5 inches in diameter and 1 inch in thickness. Refrigerate for at least 3 hours or overnight before rolling. If you plan to freeze the pie dough, do so only after the rest period of at least 3 hours in the fridge.

8. Use the dough in the recipe of your choice.

FOOD PROCESSOR METHOD

1. Keep the carrot juice in the refrigerator until step 4.

2. Put the flour, sugar, salt, and carrot powder, if using, in a food processor and pulse several times to incorporate. Sprinkle the butter cubes evenly over the surface of the dry mixture and pulse quickly 20 to 25 times to break up the cubes into smaller jaggedy pieces.

3. Turn the mixture out into a large mixing bowl. Sift through with a spatula for unprocessed butter cubes and flatten any pieces larger than a pecan half with your pointer finger and thumb.

4. Remove the carrot juice from the refrigerator. Add 2 tablespoons of the juice and stir through with a spatula. Continue adding juice 1 tablespoon at a time, pressing the dough with your hands or a spatula after each addition until it begins to come together. Avoid any heavy kneading, as overworking the dough will lead to a tough crust.

5. If the dough still has quite a bit of dry mix and doesn't hold together when a handful is squeezed, add a little more juice. Be careful not to add too much liquid (usually 3 to 5 tablespoons total are sufficient). The dough should be smooth and supple.

6. When the dough begins to hold together, turn it out onto your work surface and gently form it into a mound with your hands. Wrap the dough tightly in plastic, then gently press it into a round, flat disk, about 5 inches in diameter and 1 inch in thickness. Refrigerate for at least 3 hours or overnight before rolling. If you plan to freeze the pie dough, do so only after the rest period of at least 3 hours in the fridge.

7. Use the dough in the recipe of your choice.

CORNFLOWER PIE DOUGH
WHITE AND BLUE SPECKLE

MAKES 1 DISK OF PIE DOUGH, TO MAKE A SINGLE-CRUST PIE

½ cup ice

½ cup (118 milliliters) cold water

1¼ cups (175 grams) all-purpose flour

3 tablespoons dried blue cornflower petals

½ tablespoon granulated sugar

½ teaspoon kosher salt

½ cup (1 stick/113 grams) cold unsalted butter, cut into ½-inch cubes

I purchase food-grade dried blue cornflower petals online, and Blue Chai is my preferred brand. Be sure to pick out any outsize sepal clumps before measuring the petals for the dough dry mix.

MANUAL METHOD

1. Combine the ice and water in a small cup or bowl. Set aside.

2. Put the flour, dried cornflower petals, sugar, and salt in a large bowl and stir with a spatula to combine.

3. Sprinkle in the butter cubes and toss until each cube is coated in the flour mixture.

4. Flatten each cube of butter with your pointer fingers and thumbs. Toss again to coat the flattened butter pieces. Continue massaging the butter into the flour until the remaining shards resemble cornflakes in a range of sizes.

5. Add 2 tablespoons of the cold water, taking care not to include any ice, and fluff the moisture through the flour with a spatula. Continue adding water 1 tablespoon at a time, pressing the dough with a spatula after each addition until it begins to come together. Avoid any heavy kneading, as overworking the dough will lead to a tough crust.

6. If the dough still has quite a bit of dry mix and doesn't hold together when a handful is squeezed, add a little more water. Be careful not to add too much water (usually 3 to 5 tablespoons total are sufficient). The dough should be smooth and supple. If the dough is quite tacky, you've likely added too much liquid. Try gently incorporating a little more flour. If it is still very sticky, I suggest starting over with a new batch of ingredients. Overly hydrated dough will be difficult to roll out and utilize in these designs, and the crust will likely be tough when baked. Pie fries or pie cookies (see page 130) may be a suitable option for keeping the handling to a minimum and avoiding outright waste of the dough.

7. When the dough begins to hold together, turn it out onto your work surface and gently form it into a rounded mound with your hands. Wrap the dough tightly in plastic, then gently press it into a round, flat disk, about 5 inches in diameter and 1 inch in thickness. Refrigerate for at least 3 hours or overnight before rolling. Resting the dough in the fridge allows the gluten to relax and the dough to fully hydrate, and prevents shrinkage during baking. If you plan to freeze the pie dough, do so only after the rest period of at least 3 hours in the fridge.

8. Use the dough in the recipe of your choice.

FOOD PROCESSOR METHOD

1. Combine the ice and water in a small cup or bowl. Set aside.

2. Put the flour, dried cornflower petals, sugar, and salt in a food processor and pulse several times to incorporate. Sprinkle the butter cubes evenly over the surface of the dry mixture and pulse quickly 20 to 25 times to break up the cubes into smaller jaggedy pieces.

3. Turn the mixture out into a large mixing bowl. Sift through with a spatula for unprocessed butter cubes and flatten any pieces larger than a pecan half with your pointer finger and thumb.

4. Add 2 tablespoons of the cold water, taking care not to include any ice, and stir through with a spatula. Continue adding water 1 tablespoon at a time, pressing the dough with your hands or a spatula after each addition until it begins to come together. Avoid any heavy kneading, as overworking the dough will lead to a tough crust.

5. If the dough still has quite a bit of dry mix and doesn't hold together when a handful is squeezed, add a little more liquid. Be careful not to add too much water (usually 3 to 5 tablespoons total are sufficient). The dough should be smooth and supple. If the dough is quite tacky, you've likely added too much liquid. Try gently incorporating a little more flour. If it is still very sticky, I suggest starting over with a new batch of ingredients. Overly hydrated dough will be difficult to roll out and utilize in these designs, and the crust will likely be

recipe continues

tough when baked. Pie fries or pie cookies (see page 130) may be a suitable option for keeping the handling to a minimum and avoiding outright waste of the dough.

6. When the dough begins to hold together, turn it out onto your work surface and gently form it into a mound with your hands. Wrap the dough tightly in plastic, then gently press it into a round, flat disk, about 5 inches in diameter and 1 inch in thickness. Refrigerate for at least 3 hours or overnight before rolling. Resting the dough in the fridge allows the gluten to relax and the dough to fully hydrate, and prevents shrinkage during baking. If you plan to freeze the pie dough, do so only after the rest period of at least 3 hours in the fridge.

7. Use the dough in the recipe of your choice.

DRAGON FRUIT PIE DOUGH
HOT PINK

MAKES 1 DISK OF PIE DOUGH, TO MAKE A SINGLE-CRUST PIE

½ cup ice

½ cup (118 milliliters) cold water

1¼ cups (175 grams) all-purpose flour

2 tablespoons dragon fruit (pitaya) powder

½ tablespoon granulated sugar

½ teaspoon kosher salt

½ cup (1 stick/113 grams) cold unsalted butter, cut into ½-inch cubes

I purchase dragon fruit powder online. The coloring on dragon fruit powder can be especially variable depending on the brand. Wilderness Poets is my preferred brand.

MANUAL METHOD

1. Combine the ice and water in a small cup or bowl. Set aside.

2. Put the flour, dragon fruit powder, sugar, and salt in a large bowl and stir with a spatula to combine.

3. Sprinkle in the butter cubes and toss until each cube is coated in the flour mixture.

4. Flatten each cube of butter with your pointer fingers and thumbs. Toss again to coat the flattened butter pieces. Continue massaging the butter into the flour until the remaining shards resemble cornflakes in a range of sizes.

5. Add 2 tablespoons of the cold water, taking care not to include any ice, and fluff the moisture through the flour with a spatula. Continue adding cold water 1 tablespoon at a time, pressing the dough with a spatula after each addition until it begins to come together. Avoid any heavy kneading, as overworking the dough will lead to a tough crust.

6. If the dough still has quite a bit of dry mix and doesn't hold together when a handful is squeezed, add a little more water. Be careful not to add too much water (usually 3 to 5 tablespoons total are sufficient). The dough should be smooth and supple. If the dough is quite tacky, you've likely added too much liquid. Try gently incorporating a little more flour. If it is still very sticky, I suggest starting over with a new batch of ingredients. Overly hydrated dough will be difficult to roll out and utilize in these designs, and the crust will likely be tough when baked. Pie fries or pie cookies (see page 130) may be a suitable option for keeping the handling to a minimum and avoiding outright waste of the dough.

recipe continues

PIE DOUGHS

7. When the dough begins to hold together, turn it out onto your work surface and gently form it into a rounded mound with your hands. Wrap the dough tightly in plastic, then gently press it into a round, flat disk, about 5 inches in diameter and 1 inch in thickness. Refrigerate for at least 3 hours or overnight before rolling. Resting the dough in the fridge allows the gluten to relax and the dough to fully hydrate, and prevents shrinkage during baking. If you plan to freeze the pie dough, do so only after the rest period of at least 3 hours in the fridge.

8. Use the dough in the recipe of your choice.

FOOD PROCESSOR METHOD

1. Combine the ice and water in a small cup or bowl. Set aside.

2. Put the flour, dragon fruit powder, sugar, and salt in a food processor and pulse several times to incorporate. Sprinkle the butter cubes evenly over the surface of the dry mixture and pulse quickly 20 to 25 times to break up the cubes into smaller jaggedy pieces.

3. Turn the mixture out into a large mixing bowl. Sift through with a spatula for unprocessed butter cubes and flatten any pieces larger than a pecan half with your pointer finger and thumb.

4. Add 2 tablespoons of the cold water, taking care not to include any ice, and stir through with a spatula. Continue adding water 1 tablespoon at a time, pressing the dough with your hands or a spatula between each addition until it begins to come together. Avoid any heavy kneading, as overworking the dough will lead to a tough crust.

5. If the dough still has quite a bit of dry mix and doesn't hold together when a handful is squeezed, add a little more water. Be careful not to add too much water (usually 3 to 5 tablespoons total are sufficient). The dough should be smooth and supple. If the dough is quite tacky, you've likely added too much water. Try gently incorporating a little more flour. If it is still very sticky, I suggest starting over with a new batch of ingredients. Overly hydrated dough will be difficult to roll out and utilize in these designs, and the crust will likely be tough when baked. Pie fries or pie cookies (see page 130) may

be a suitable option for keeping the handling to a minimum and avoiding outright waste of the dough.

6. When the dough begins to hold together, turn it out onto your work surface and gently form it into a mound with your hands. Wrap the dough tightly in plastic, then gently press it into a round, flat disk, about 5 inches in diameter and 1 inch in thickness. Refrigerate for at least 3 hours or overnight before rolling. Resting the dough in the fridge allows the gluten to relax and the dough to fully hydrate, and prevents shrinkage during baking. If you plan to freeze the pie dough, do so only after the rest period of at least 3 hours in the fridge.

7. Use the dough in the recipe of your choice.

NUTELLA PIE DOUGH
BROWN MARBLE

MAKES 1 DISK OF PIE DOUGH, TO MAKE A SINGLE-CRUST PIE

½ cup ice

½ cup (118 milliliters) cold water

1¼ cups (175 grams) all-purpose flour

½ teaspoon kosher salt

½ cup (1 stick/113 grams) cold unsalted butter, cut into ½-inch cubes

2 tablespoons (37 grams) Nutella, frozen and cut into ½-inch chunks

NOTE: Since the Nutella gets warm and sticky quickly, this dough is not recommended for the string art–inspired or woven designs that require more time and manipulation.

MANUAL METHOD

1. Combine the ice and water in a small cup or bowl. Set aside.

2. Put the flour and salt in a large bowl and stir with a spatula to combine.

3. Sprinkle in the butter cubes and Nutella chunks, and toss until coated in the flour mixture.

4. Flatten each cube of butter and Nutella with your pointer fingers and thumbs. Toss again to coat the flattened pieces. Working quickly, continue massaging the butter and Nutella into the flour until the remaining shards resemble cornflakes in a range of sizes.

5. Add 2 tablespoons of the cold water, taking care not to include any ice, and fluff the moisture through the flour with a spatula. Continue adding cold water 1 tablespoon at a time, pressing the dough with a spatula after each addition until it begins to come together. Avoid any heavy kneading, as overworking the dough will lead to a tough crust.

6. If the dough still has quite a bit of dry mix and doesn't hold together when a handful is squeezed, add a little more water. Be careful not to add too much water (usually 3 to 5 tablespoons total are sufficient). The dough should be smooth and supple. If the dough is quite tacky, you've likely added too much liquid. Try gently incorporating a little more flour. If it is still very sticky, I suggest starting over with a new batch of ingredients. Overly hydrated dough will be difficult to roll out and utilize in these designs, and the crust will likely be tough when baked. Pie fries or pie cookies (see page 130) may be a suitable option for keeping the handling to a minimum and avoiding outright waste of the dough.

7. When the dough begins to hold together, turn it out onto your work surface and gently form it into a rounded mound with your hands. Wrap the dough tightly in plastic, then gently press it into a round, flat disk, about 5 inches in diameter and 1 inch in thickness. Refrigerate for at least 3 hours or overnight before rolling. Resting the dough in the fridge allows the gluten to relax and the dough to fully hydrate, and prevents shrinkage during baking. If you plan to freeze the pie dough, do so only after the rest period of at least 3 hours in the fridge.

8. Use the dough in the recipe of your choice.

FOOD PROCESSOR METHOD

1. Combine the ice and water in a small cup or bowl. Set aside.

2. Put the flour and salt in a food processor and pulse several times to incorporate. Sprinkle the butter cubes and Nutella chunks evenly over the surface of the dry mixture and pulse quickly 20 to 25 times to break up the cubes into smaller jaggedy pieces.

3. Turn the mixture out into a large mixing bowl. Sift through with a spatula for unprocessed butter cubes and Nutella chunks and flatten any pieces larger than a pecan half with your pointer finger and thumb.

4. Add 2 tablespoons of the cold water, taking care not to include any ice, and stir through with a spatula. Continue adding water 1 tablespoon at a time, pressing the dough with your hands or a spatula after each addition until it begins to come together. Avoid any heavy kneading, as overworking the dough will lead to a tough crust.

5. If the dough still has quite a bit of dry mix and doesn't hold together when a handful is squeezed, add a little more water. Be careful not to add too much water (usually 3 to 5 tablespoons total are sufficient). The dough should be smooth and supple. If the dough is quite tacky, you've likely added too much water. Try gently incorporating a little more flour. If it is still very sticky, I suggest starting over with a new batch of ingredients. Overly hydrated dough will be difficult to roll out and utilize in these designs, and the crust will likely be

recipe continues

tough when baked. Pie fries or pie cookies (see page 130) may be a suitable option for keeping the handling to a minimum and avoiding outright waste of the dough.

6. When the dough begins to hold together, turn it out onto your work surface and gently form it into a mound with your hands. Wrap the dough tightly in plastic, then gently press it into a round, flat disk, about 5 inches in diameter and 1 inch in thickness. Refrigerate for at least 3 hours or overnight before rolling. Resting the dough in the fridge allows the gluten to relax and the dough to fully hydrate, and prevents shrinkage during baking. If you plan to freeze the pie dough, do so only after the rest period of at least 3 hours in the fridge.

7. Use the dough in the recipe of your choice.

MARBLED PIE DOUGH

Some designs do not utilize the full disks of dough called for in a recipe, and you may have extra strips, shapes, or scraps. These can be gently pressed together into a disk, wrapped in plastic, and chilled for at least 1 hour in the fridge before rolling. To avoid flavor cacophony, scraps of Nutella Dough and/or Whole Wheat Cheddar Chive Dough are not recommended for this. Otherwise, any combination of scraps from leftover Basic, Beet, Black Sesame, Blueberry, Butterfly Pea Flower, Carrot, Cornflower, Dragon Fruit, and Spinach doughs will roll beautifully into a galaxy or tie-dye-like canvas.

SPINACH PIE DOUGH
GREEN

MAKES 1 DISK OF PIE DOUGH, TO MAKE A SINGLE-CRUST PIE

1¼ cups (175 grams) all-purpose flour

½ teaspoon kosher salt

½ tablespoon poppy seeds (optional)

½ cup (1 stick/113 grams) cold unsalted butter, cut into ½-inch cubes

½ cup (118 milliliters) cold fresh spinach juice (see page 164)

MANUAL METHOD

1. Keep the spinach juice in the refrigerator until step 5.

2. Put the flour, salt, and poppy seeds, if using, in a large bowl and stir with a spatula to combine.

3. Sprinkle in the butter cubes and toss until each cube is coated in the flour mixture.

4. Flatten each cube of butter with your pointer fingers and thumbs. Toss again to coat the flattened butter pieces. Continue massaging the butter into the flour until the remaining shards resemble cornflakes in a range of sizes.

5. Remove the spinach juice from the refrigerator. Add 2 tablespoons of the juice and fluff the moisture through the flour with a spatula. Continue adding juice 1 tablespoon at a time, pressing the dough with a spatula after each addition until it begins to come together. Avoid any heavy kneading, as overworking the dough will lead to a tough crust.

6. If the dough still has quite a bit of dry mix and doesn't hold together when a handful is squeezed, add a little more juice. Be careful not to add too much liquid (usually 3 to 5 tablespoons total are sufficient). The dough should be smooth and supple. If the dough is quite tacky, you've likely added too much liquid. Try gently incorporating a little more flour. If it is still very sticky, I suggest starting over with a new batch of ingredients. Overly hydrated dough will be difficult to roll out and utilize in these designs, and the crust will likely be tough when baked. Pie fries or pie cookies (see page 130) may be a suitable option for keeping the handling to a minimum and avoiding outright waste of the dough.

7. When the dough begins to hold together, turn it out onto your work surface and gently form it into a rounded mound with your hands. Wrap the dough tightly in plastic, then gently press it into a round, flat disk, about 5 inches in diameter and 1 inch in thickness. Refrigerate for at least 3 hours or

overnight before rolling. Resting the dough in the fridge allows the gluten to relax and the dough to fully hydrate, and prevents shrinkage during baking. If you plan to freeze the pie dough, do so only after the rest period of at least 3 hours in the fridge.

8. Use the dough in the recipe of your choice.

FOOD PROCESSOR METHOD

1. Keep the spinach juice in the refrigerator until step 4.

2. Put the flour, salt, and poppy seeds, if using, in a food processor and pulse several times to incorporate. Sprinkle the butter cubes evenly over the surface of the dry mixture and pulse quickly 20 to 25 times to break up the cubes into smaller jaggedy pieces.

3. Turn the mixture out into a large mixing bowl. Sift through with a spatula for unprocessed butter cubes and flatten any pieces larger than a pecan half with your pointer finger and thumb.

4. Remove the spinach juice from the refrigerator. Add 2 tablespoons of the juice and stir through with a spatula. Continue adding juice 1 tablespoon at a time, pressing the dough with your hands or a spatula after each addition until it begins to come together. Avoid any heavy kneading, as overworking the dough will lead to a tough crust.

5. If the dough still has quite a bit of dry mix and doesn't hold together when a handful is squeezed, add a little more juice. Be careful not to add too much liquid (usually 3 to 5 tablespoons total are sufficient). The dough should be smooth and supple. If the dough is quite tacky, you've likely added too much liquid. Try gently incorporating a little more flour. If it is still very sticky, I suggest starting over with a new batch of ingredients. Overly hydrated dough will be difficult to roll out and utilize in these designs, and the crust will likely be tough when baked. Pie fries or pie cookies (see page 130) may be a suitable option for keeping the handling to a minimum and avoiding outright waste of the dough.

6. When the dough begins to hold together, turn it out onto your work surface and gently form it into a mound with your

recipe continues

hands. Wrap the dough tightly in plastic, then gently press it into a round, flat disk, about 5 inches in diameter and 1 inch in thickness. Refrigerate for at least 3 hours or overnight before rolling. Resting the dough in the fridge allows the gluten to relax and the dough to fully hydrate, and prevents shrinkage during baking. If you plan to freeze the pie dough, do so only after the rest period of at least 3 hours in the fridge.

7. Use the dough in the recipe of your choice.

SPINACH JUICE

½ pound fresh baby spinach

BLENDER METHOD (MAKES ABOUT ¾ CUP/177 MILLILITERS)

1. Combine the spinach and ½ cup (118 milliliters) water in a blender and puree until smooth.

2. Pass the mixture through a fine-mesh sieve, pressing the pulp with a spatula to extract as much liquid as possible. Discard the pulp and pass the liquid through the sieve one additional time.

3. Chill the juice in the refrigerator until cold before using.

ELECTRIC JUICER METHOD (MAKES JUST OVER ½ CUP/118 MILLILITERS)

1. Run the spinach through an electric juicer. Discard the remaining pulp and pass the juice through a fine-mesh sieve twice. Skim off any residual foam.

2. Chill the juice in the refrigerator until cold before using.

WHOLE WHEAT CHEDDAR CHIVE PIE DOUGH
TAN SPECKLE

MAKES 1 DISK OF PIE DOUGH, TO MAKE A SINGLE-CRUST PIE

½ cup ice

½ cup (118 milliliters) cold water

2 ounces (56 grams) sharp Cheddar cheese, grated and finely chopped

¼ cup (36 grams) all-purpose flour

1 cup (142 grams) whole wheat flour

2 tablespoons (0.25 ounce/6 grams) finely chopped fresh chives

½ teaspoon kosher salt

½ cup (1 stick/113 grams) cold unsalted butter, cut into ½-inch cubes

MANUAL METHOD

1. Combine the ice and water in a small cup or bowl. Set aside.

2. Put the cheese, flours, chives, and salt in a large bowl and stir with a spatula to combine.

3. Sprinkle in the butter cubes and toss until each cube is coated in the flour mixture.

4. Flatten each cube of butter with your pointer fingers and thumbs. Toss again to coat the flattened butter pieces. Continue massaging the butter into the flour until the remaining shards resemble cornflakes in a range of sizes.

5. Add 2 tablespoons of the cold water, taking care not to include any ice, and fluff the moisture through the flour with a spatula. Continue adding water 1 tablespoon at a time, pressing the dough with a spatula after each addition until it begins to come together. Avoid any heavy kneading, as overworking the dough will lead to a tough crust.

6. If the dough still has quite a bit of dry mix and doesn't hold together when a handful is squeezed, add a little more water. Be careful not to add too much water (usually 3 to 5 tablespoons total are sufficient). The dough should be smooth and supple. If the dough is quite tacky, you've likely added too much liquid. Try gently incorporating a little more flour. If it is still very sticky, I suggest starting over with a new batch of ingredients. Overly hydrated dough will be difficult to roll out and utilize in these designs, and the crust will likely be tough when baked. Pie fries or pie cookies (see page 130) may be a suitable option for keeping the handling to a minimum and avoiding outright waste of the dough.

7. When the dough begins to hold together, turn it out onto your work surface and gently form it into a rounded mound with your hands. Wrap the dough tightly in plastic, then gently press it into a round, flat disk, about 5 inches in diameter

recipe continues

and 1 inch in thickness. Refrigerate for at least 3 hours or overnight before rolling. Resting the dough in the fridge allows the gluten to relax and the dough to fully hydrate, and prevents shrinkage during baking. If you plan to freeze the pie dough, do so only after the rest period of at least 3 hours in the fridge.

8. Use the dough in the recipe of your choice.

FOOD PROCESSOR METHOD

1. Combine the ice and water in a small cup or bowl. Set aside.

2. Put the cheese, flours, chives, and salt in a food processor and pulse several times to incorporate. Sprinkle the butter cubes evenly over the surface of the dry mixture and pulse quickly 20 to 25 times to break up the cubes into smaller jaggedy pieces.

3. Turn the mixture out into a large mixing bowl. Sift through with a spatula for unprocessed butter cubes and flatten any pieces larger than a pecan half with your pointer finger and thumb.

4. Add 2 tablespoons of the cold water, taking care not to include any ice, and stir through with a spatula. Continue adding water 1 tablespoon at a time, pressing the dough with your hands or a spatula after each addition until it begins to come together. Avoid any heavy kneading, as overworking the dough will lead to a tough crust.

5. If the dough still has quite a bit of dry mix and doesn't hold together when a handful is squeezed, add a little more liquid. Be careful not to add too much water (usually 3 to 5 tablespoons total are sufficient). The dough should be smooth and supple. If the dough is quite tacky, you've likely added too much liquid. Try gently incorporating a little more flour. If it is still very sticky, I suggest starting over with a new batch of ingredients. Overly hydrated dough will be difficult to roll out and utilize in these designs, and the crust will likely be tough when baked. Pie fries or pie cookies (see page 130) may be a suitable option for keeping the handling to a minimum and avoiding outright waste of the dough.

6. When the dough begins to hold together, turn it out onto your work surface and gently form it into a mound with your hands. Wrap the dough tightly in plastic, then gently press it into a round, flat disk, about 5 inches in diameter and 1 inch in thickness. Refrigerate for at least 3 hours or overnight before rolling. Resting the dough in the fridge allows the gluten to relax and the dough to fully hydrate, and prevents shrinkage during baking. If you plan to freeze the pie dough, do so only after the rest period of at least 3 hours in the fridge.

7. Use the dough in the recipe of your choice.

PIE DESIGNS

CURLS OF WISDOM

I was babysitting four-year-old twins on an overnight and we were all in the bathroom brushing teeth before bed. Kate saw my razor resting in the shower caddy and looked at me incredulously.

"You have a mustache?!"

Her sister, Lauren, rolled her eyes, and responded, "No, silly! That's for her eyebrows!"

So, if you're in the market for grooming advice, I know some people. As for wisdom relating to any other regimen, I'd stick to Google, though word on the street is that consuming this pie evokes a state of enlightenment. The white carrot filling is reminiscent of a light cheesecake with its creamy texture. The savory notes of the miso, not unlike precocious twins, light up the party with unexpected jocularity. Combined with the nutty, crunchy black sesame crust, the whole experience is revelatory.

2 disks Black Sesame Pie Dough (page 141)

MISO WHITE CARROT FILLING

1 pound (454 grams) white carrots, peeled and roughly chopped (see filling alternatives, page 172)

1 cup (237 milliliters) heavy cream

3 tablespoons (42 grams) unsalted butter, melted and cooled

½ cup (99 grams) granulated sugar

2 tablespoons (36 grams) white miso

2 large eggs

TEXTURED CURLS DESIGN NEEDS

Parchment paper

1-inch oval cutter

1. On a floured surface, roll 1 dough disk into a 14-inch circle. Roll the dough onto the rolling pin and unfurl it over a 9-inch pie pan. Taking the edges of the dough, gently ease the dough in, nestling it into the inner elbows of the pie pan. Stretched dough contributes to shrinkage during the baking process, so take care not to forcefully pull the dough into the corners of the pan. Trim the excess dough with kitchen shears to create a 1-inch overhang. Fold the overhang back under, creating an elevated edge. Crimp the dough all the way around the pie edge.

2. Freeze the pie shell solid, about 20 minutes.

3. Preheat the oven to 350°F.

4. To blind-bake, line the pie shell tightly with foil. Fill to the top with pie weights and place on a rimmed baking sheet. Bake for 25 to 27 minutes, until the foil no longer sticks to the dough. Remove the foil and pie weights and bake until the crust is crisp and opaque, 10 to 15 minutes.

5. Put the carrots in a small saucepan, cover with water, and boil until fork-tender.

6. Drain the carrots and puree them in a food processor until smooth. Add the heavy cream, butter, sugar, and miso and process until smooth. Add the eggs and pulse until just combined.

recipe continues

7. Pour the miso white carrot filling into the partially baked shell, jiggling the pan slightly to smooth the top and eliminate any bubbles. Bake until the filling is just set, 40 to 50 minutes, covering the edges with a shield as necessary. The center of the pie should retain a slight jiggle.

8. While the pie is baking, on a floured surface, roll the second dough disk into a 12-inch circle. Roll the dough onto the rolling pin and unfurl it onto a sheet of parchment paper. Using a 1-inch oval cutter, punch out 25 shapes. Using the curved edge of the oval cutter, cut each oval into 3 or 4 banana-shaped sections. Separate the dough pieces on the sheet of parchment.

9. Slide a flat baking sheet under the parchment and chill the dough in the refrigerator for at least 10 minutes.

10. Bake the dough curls (still at 350°F) for 10 to 15 minutes, until crisp. Arrange the baked curls across the surface of the baked pie in a random, scattered pattern to create a textured effect.

11. Serve the pie chilled or at room temperature.

SUGGESTED SUBSTITUTIONS

Dough alternatives: The Black Sesame dough pairs really well with this filling, but Beet (page 138), Blueberry (page 144), Butterfly Pea Flower (page 147), Carrot (page 150), Cornflower (page 152), or Dragon Fruit (page 155) dough can be substituted. Any portion of leftover dough is especially well suited for creating the curl topping.

Filling alternatives: I purchase bunches of rainbow carrots, from which I pull the white ones. While orange carrots can be used to no detriment, the subtler flavor of the white carrots is ideal.

NOTE

This pie does not freeze well. Store any leftovers well sealed in the refrigerator and consume within 3 days.

ONCE IN A TILE

In a face-off between Team Apple and Team Pumpkin, I fully advocate for apple. But swirl some black tahini into the pumpkin puree and suddenly I'm entertaining treasonous thoughts about hopping on gourd with the squash contingent instead. This twist on a very traditional flavor is sure to pump up some controversy, but what's a little healthy competition among pie-vals once in a while?

2 disks Black Sesame Pie Dough (page 141)

PUMPKIN BLACK SESAME FILLING

One 15-ounce can pumpkin puree (not pumpkin pie filling)

One 14-ounce can sweetened condensed milk

2 large eggs

1 teaspoon ground cinnamon

½ teaspoon ground ginger

½ teaspoon grated nutmeg

¼ teaspoon ground cloves

¼ teaspoon ground allspice

½ teaspoon kosher salt

3 tablespoons black tahini (see page 13)

TRIANGLE TILE DESIGN NEEDS

Parchment paper

1-inch square cutter

Paring knife

1. On a floured surface, roll 1 dough disk into a 14-inch circle. Roll the dough onto the rolling pin and unfurl it over a 9-inch pie pan. Taking the edges of the dough, gently ease the dough into the pan, nestling it into the inner elbows of the pie pan. Trim the excess dough with kitchen shears to create a 1-inch overhang. Fold the overhang back under, creating an elevated edge. Crimp the dough all the way around the pie edge.

2. Freeze the pie shell solid, about 20 minutes.

3. Preheat the oven to 350°F.

4. To blind-bake, line the pie shell tightly with foil. Fill to the top with pie weights and place on a rimmed baking sheet. Bake for 25 to 27 minutes, until the foil no longer sticks to the dough. Remove the foil and pie weights and bake until the crust is crisp and opaque, 10 to 15 minutes. Leave the oven on at 350°F and proceed with preparing the filling.

5. In a large bowl, combine the pumpkin puree, condensed milk, eggs, cinnamon, ginger, nutmeg, cloves, allspice, and salt. Whisk well.

6. Scoop 1 cup of the pumpkin mixture into a small bowl and add the black tahini. Whisk well.

7. Place the pie pan on a rimmed baking sheet. Spread the pumpkin black tahini mixture evenly in the pie shell. Gently spoon the pumpkin filling on top to make a second layer and jiggle the pie slightly to smooth the surface. Use a paring knife to poke away any bubbles.

8. Bake the pie until the filling is just set, 40 to 50 minutes, covering the edges with a shield as necessary. The center of the pie should retain a slight jiggle.

recipe continues

9. While the pie is baking, on a floured surface, roll the second dough disk into a 12-inch square. Roll the dough onto the rolling pin and unfurl it onto a sheet of parchment paper. Using a 1-inch square cutter, punch out at least 40 squares and place them on a separate sheet of parchment. Cut each square into quarters on the diagonals with a paring knife to create four isosceles (right) triangles. Arrange the triangles on the parchment so they are not touching.

10. Slide a flat baking sheet under the parchment and chill the dough in the refrigerator for at least 10 minutes.

11. Bake the dough triangles (still at 350°F) for 10 to 15 minutes, until crisp.

12. When the pie and triangles have cooled slightly, lay a ruler horizontally across the center of the pie, resting on the pie crust edges. Starting from the left edge of the pie, line the long side of one baked triangle against the ruler and place another piece in its mirror image above it. Moving right, place two more triangles like the first two but rotated 90 degrees. Repeat the configuration of the first two triangles and continue down the row two triangles at a time, alternating the placement.

13. When the first row has been completed, lay a second row of triangles below, staggering the placement. While all the

triangles should touch corners, the sides of the triangles should align only with the pumpkin pie negative space. Continue placing triangles row by row until the entire surface of the pie has been covered.

14. Serve the pie chilled or at room temperature.

SUGGESTED SUBSTITUTIONS

Dough alternatives: Basic (page 134), Beet (page 138), Dragon Fruit (page 155)

NOTE

This pie does not freeze well. Store any leftovers well sealed in the refrigerator and consume within 3 days.

Thanks to a traumatic near-death experience in early childhood, I spent most of my life terrified of dogs and wary of animals in general. Ben, ever the optimist, spent eleven years subjecting me to puppy photos from the Internet and slowly inculcating me with canine facts until I acquiesced and agreed to consider a pet.

After several meet and greets, and no small amount of uncertainty on my part, we brought home Santi, a Shar-Pei/bear/hippopotamus/capybara/warthog hybrid rescue, and what do you know? He is the great love of my life. Regular features of his downy snoot in my

Instagram stories have resulted in his own loyal following, and I cannot remember life before him.

As with dogs, I've always been doubtful of bananas and what they bring to the table. But they're Santi's all-time favorite treat, and his enthusiasm for the things he loves is hard to escape. This malted banana cream pie piled high with whipped cream and topped with crispy morsels is my ode to the fuzzy puddle of wrinkles that changed my perspective on so many things, dogs and bananas included. I hope you love it as much as I love Santi.

2 disks Nutella Pie Dough (page 158)

MALTED CHOCOLATE PUDDING

2 egg yolks

2¼ cups (533 milliliters) milk

½ cup (56 grams) malted milk powder

¼ cup (50 grams) granulated sugar

2 tablespoons (11 grams) unsweetened Dutch-process cocoa powder

2 tablespoons (15 grams) cornstarch

1. On a floured surface, roll 1 dough disk into a 14-inch circle. Roll the dough onto the rolling pin and unfurl it over a 9-inch pie pan. Taking the edges of the dough, gently ease the dough into the pan, nestling it into the inner elbows of the pie pan. Trim the excess dough with kitchen shears to create a 1-inch overhang. Fold the overhang back under, creating an elevated edge. Crimp the dough all the way around the pie edge.

2. Freeze the pie shell solid, about 20 minutes. The pie shell can be wrapped and kept frozen for up to 3 months.

3. Preheat the oven to 350°F.

4. To blind-bake, line the pie shell tightly with foil. Fill to the top with pie weights and place on a rimmed baking sheet. Bake for 25 to 27 minutes, until the foil no longer sticks to the dough. Remove the foil and pie weights and bake until the crust is crisp and cooked through, 10 to 15 minutes. Cool completely before filling.

recipe continues

PIE DESIGNS

½ teaspoon kosher salt

2 ounces (56 grams) bittersweet chocolate, finely chopped

MALTED WHIPPED CREAM

2 tablespoons (14 grams) malted milk powder

2 tablespoons (14 grams) powdered sugar

1 cup (237 milliliters) heavy cream

3 large bananas, peeled and sliced into ¼-inch rounds

FEATHER DESIGN NEEDS

Parchment paper

1-inch rhombus cutter

Paring knife

5. To make the malted chocolate pudding, whisk the egg yolks and ¼ cup (59 milliliters) of the milk in a small bowl. Set aside.

6. Sift the malted milk powder, sugar, cocoa powder, cornstarch, and salt into a 2-quart saucepan. With the pan over medium heat, drizzle in the remaining 2 cups (474 milliliters) milk, whisking constantly. When the mixture begins to thicken, add the chocolate and whisk until melted and fully incorporated. Slowly drizzle in the egg mixture, still whisking constantly, and let the mixture come to a lively boil.

7. Pass the mixture through a fine-mesh sieve, cover the surface with plastic wrap to prevent a skin from forming, and chill in the refrigerator. The pudding should be cold when the pie is assembled.

8. To make the malted whipped cream, sift the malted milk powder and powdered sugar into a medium bowl. Pour in the heavy cream and whip to stiff peaks with an electric mixer.

9. Chill both the pudding and the whipped cream in the refrigerator until you are ready to assemble the pie.

10. Preheat the oven to 350°F. Lay a sheet of parchment paper on an unrimmed baking sheet.

11. On a floured surface, roll the second disk of dough into a 14-inch circle. Using a 1-inch rhombus cutter, punch out 85 shapes. Space the shapes on the parchment and bake for 15 to 20 minutes, until crisp and flaky.

12. Line the baked pie shell with a layer of banana slices. Spoon half of the chilled malted chocolate pudding over the bananas and top with another layer of banana slices. Pour in the remaining chocolate pudding and smooth the surface. Scoop the whipped cream evenly over the surface, using an offset spatula to create a few swirls and swoops. Stick the baked rhombi into the whipped cream row by row in an overlapping shingle-like fashion.

13. Keep the pie in the refrigerator until ready to serve. This pie is best consumed within 2 days.

Dough alternatives: This is a great occasion to use up extra portions of dough from other designs. Substitute 1 disk colored dough, or any other extra dough, for 1 disk of the Nutella dough for the feathered cutouts.

NOTE

Freezing is not recommended for this pie. Keep in the refrigerator and consume within 3 days.

MOTHER OF SWIRL

Besides reading under the covers when I was supposed to be sleeping, my favorite hobby growing up was hula-hooping. I would stand on our front lawn for hours, hooping until sundown. I couldn't do any fancy tricks and I never managed to twirl more than one at a time, but it was a soothing diversion nonetheless.

Constructing this nut swirl feels similarly simple and meditative. Whether you choose to create an intricate mosaic with an assortment of nut pieces or a straightforward spiral of whole nuts, swirling has never been more hip.

1 disk Dragon Fruit Pie Dough (page 155)

SPICY MAPLE NUT FILLING

1 cup (5 ounces/146 grams) unsalted peanuts

1 cup (4 ounces/115 grams) pecan halves

1 cup (4 ounces/115 grams) walnuts

1 cup (322 grams) pure maple syrup

⅔ cup (132 grams) packed light brown sugar

1 teaspoon cayenne

1 teaspoon kosher salt

1 teaspoon fresh lemon juice

6 tablespoons (¾ stick/85 grams) unsalted butter, melted and cooled

3 large eggs, lightly whisked

NUT MOSAIC DESIGN NEEDS

½ cup (2 ounces/56 grams) pecan halves

½ cup (3 ounces) pepitas (hulled raw pumpkin seeds)

1. On a floured surface, roll the dough disk into a 14-inch circle. Roll the dough onto the rolling pin and unfurl it over a 9-inch pie pan. Taking the edges of the dough, gently ease the dough into the pan, nestling it into the inner elbows of the pie pan. Trim the excess dough with kitchen shears to create a 1-inch overhang. Fold the overhang back under, creating an elevated edge. Crimp the dough all the way around the pie edge.

2. Freeze the pie shell solid, about 20 minutes.

3. Preheat the oven to 350°F.

4. To make the spicy maple nut filling, spread the nuts in a single layer on a rimmed baking sheet and toast for 10 to 12 minutes, until fragrant. Cool slightly and roughly chop. Set aside.

5. In a medium bowl, whisk the maple syrup, brown sugar, cayenne, salt, lemon juice, and melted butter. Pour in the eggs and gently stir the mixture with a spatula until just combined. Do not overmix. Add the toasted nuts and stir gently to coat.

6. Pour the nut mixture into the pie shell.

7. Place the pecan halves in a mosaic-style spiral shape on the surface of the pie. Sprinkle the pepitas into the negative space to create a duo-toned spiral design.

8. Place the pie on a rimmed baking sheet and bake until the filling is just set, 40 to 50 minutes, covering the edges with a shield as necessary. The center of the pie should retain a slight jiggle.

9. Cool the pie completely before serving.

recipe continues

Dough alternatives: Basic (page 134), Beet (page 138), Black Sesame (page 141), Blueberry (page 144), Butterfly Pea Flower (page 147), Nutella (page 158)

Dough alternatives: Basic (page 134), Beet (page 138), Black Sesame (page 141), Blueberry (page 144), Butterfly Pea Flower (page 147), Nutella (page 158)

NOTE

Freezing is not recommended for this pie. Keep in the refrigerator and consume within 3 days.

C AND EASY

Every November, we host a Friendsgiving, where we congregate what feels like everyone we know in the city and attempt to cram them all inside our house at one long table. It's usually a boisterous midmorning brunch situation, and everyone contributes a fall-inspired dish or beverage. There are always too many provisions and never enough waistband on our stretchy pants.

One year, there was a harvest Bloody Mary bar that took up our entire bookshelf and four different kinds of macaroni and cheese. This pie was an innovation of repurposed leftover scoops of pasta, and it has since become a Friendsgiving fixture.

Call your chums over to annihilate this with you, or shovel it down with your bare hands, crumbs flying and no one around to see. Be free. It's easy as A, B . . . C.

2 disks Whole Wheat Cheddar Chive Pie Dough (page 165)

BUTTERNUT BACON MAC AND CHEESE FILLING

1 pound (454 grams) butternut squash, peeled and cut into ½-inch cubes

1 tablespoon olive oil

1 teaspoon kosher salt, plus more to taste

½ teaspoon freshly ground black pepper, plus more to taste

½ pound (227 grams) thick-cut bacon, chopped

8 ounces (114 grams) uncooked elbow macaroni noodles

1 tablespoon (14 grams) unsalted butter

1 tablespoon (9 grams) flour

1. On a floured surface, roll 1 dough disk into a 14-inch circle. Roll the dough onto the rolling pin and unfurl it onto a sheet of parchment paper. Using a ruler as a straight line guide, punch out a column of C's, spaced 1 inch apart, with a letter cutter down the center of the dough. Punch out a row of inverted C's, interlocking the shapes with the first row. Continue until the entire surface of the pie crust has been covered with approximately 9 vertical rows of interlocking letters.

2. Slide a flat baking sheet under the parchment and place the perforated pie top in the freezer until frozen solid, about 20 minutes.

3. Preheat the oven to 375°F. Line a rimmed baking sheet with foil.

4. Toss the butternut squash cubes with the oil, salt, and pepper and arrange them in a single layer on the prepared baking sheet. Roast until tender, about 35 minutes. Puree the roasted butternut squash in a food processor until smooth.

5. While the squash is in the oven, cook the bacon in a skillet until crisp and drain on a paper towel–lined plate. Set aside.

6. Cook the macaroni in a large pot of salted water for 2 minutes less than directed on the package. The macaroni should be just short of al dente. Drain and set aside.

recipe continues

1 cup (237 milliliters) milk

4 ounces (57 grams) sharp Cheddar cheese, grated (about 1 cup)

Egg wash (see page 130)

MACARONI CUTOUT DESIGN NEEDS

Parchment paper

Ruler

1-inch letter C cutter

Paring knife

7. In the same pot, melt the butter over medium heat and sprinkle in the flour, whisking constantly until the roux has darkened to a deep brown. Slowly drizzle in the milk while continuing to whisk and cook to warm through. Add the cheese and whisk until melted and smooth. Stir in the squash puree, then the cooked pasta and bacon. Season with salt and pepper and remove from the heat.

8. Turn the oven up to 400°F.

9. Roll the second dough disk into a 14-inch circle. Roll the dough onto the rolling pin and unfurl it over a 9-inch pie pan. Taking the edges of the dough, gently ease the dough into the pan, nestling it into the inner elbows of the pie pan. Scoop the cooked filling into the pie shell, smoothing the surface. Use a small pastry brush to lightly dab water around the edge of the dough.

10. Remove the frozen pie top from the freezer and lay it on the surface of the filled pie. Let it sit for a few minutes to thaw slightly and settle. Seal and crimp the edges or trim with a paring knife to create a sharp edge.

11. Place the entire pie on a rimmed baking sheet, brush with egg wash, and bake until the crust is golden and crispy, 45 to 55 minutes.

SUGGESTED SUBSTITUTIONS

Dough alternatives: Basic (page 134), Carrot (page 150), Spinach (page 162)

NOTES

Use the pointy end of a chopstick to gently nudge the dough out of the letter cutter onto a sheet of parchment. These can be baked off as crackers (see page 130).

While this pie is best when baked right away, it can be frozen up to 1 month before baking. Seal well before freezing.

EASY ON THE I'S

There are plenty of fakes out there—counterfeit money, knock-off Vouis Luitton handbags, imitation crab. Now fake lattice can join the shrewd ranks of imposters, too. There's no forgery or surgical augmentation required to achieve this classic basket motif, and best of all, no actual weaving, either! With a mere sleight of hand, you too can produce a copycat lattice to auction on the black market. Just remember to I low and sell pie.

2 disks Butterfly Pea Flower Pie Dough (page 147)

NECTARINE BLACKBERRY FILLING

2 pounds (907 grams/ about 6) nectarines, pitted and cut into 1-inch chunks

2 cups (11 ounces/ 312 grams) fresh or frozen blackberries

1 cup (198 grams) granulated sugar

⅓ cup (38 grams) tapioca starch

1 teaspoon kosher salt

½ teaspoon grated nutmeg

FAKE LATTICE DESIGN NEEDS

Parchment paper

Letter I cutter

Paring knife

1. On a floured surface, roll 1 dough disk into a 13-inch circle. Roll the dough onto the rolling pin and unfurl it onto a sheet of parchment paper. Punch out a patterned row, alternating between 3 vertical I's and 3 horizontal I's, using a ruler as a straight line guide.

2. Slide a flat baking sheet under the parchment and place the perforated pie top in the freezer until frozen solid, about 20 minutes.

3. Roll the second dough disk into a 14-inch circle. Roll the dough onto the rolling pin and unfurl it over a 9-inch pie pan. Taking the edges of the dough, gently ease the dough into the tin, nestling it into the inner elbows of the pie pan. Trim the excess dough with kitchen shears to create a 1-inch overhang. Fold the overhang back under, creating an elevated edge.

4. To make the nectarine blackberry filling, combine all the ingredients in a large bowl and gently fold with a spatula to coat the fruit in the dry mix.

5. Scoop the filling into the pie shell. Use a small pastry brush to lightly dab water around the edge of the dough.

6. Remove the frozen pie top from the freezer, pick it up as one solid piece, and lay it centered on the surface of your filled pie. Let it sit for a few minutes to thaw slightly and settle. Press to seal the edges and trim with a paring knife to create a clean edge.

7. Chill the entire pie in the freezer until the oven has come to temperature. The pie can be frozen until solid before baking or simply chilled through, about 20 minutes.

8. Preheat the oven to 400°F. Line a rimmed baking sheet with parchment.

9. When the oven comes to temperature, remove the pie from the freezer and place it on the prepared baking sheet.

10. Bake for 25 minutes, then rotate the pie 180 degrees and lower the oven temperature to 350°F. If the edges are already brown, cover with a shield. If the top begins to brown excessively, rest a sheet of foil lightly on top. Continue baking until the filling is bubbling in the center, checking every 30 minutes to rotate the pie and adjust the shields as necessary, 75 to 90 total minutes. (If baking from frozen, add 30 to 45 minutes to the bake time.)

11. Cool the pie completely on a rack before slicing and serving.

SUGGESTED SUBSTITUTIONS

Dough alternatives: Basic (page 134), Beet (page 138), Black Sesame (page 141), Blueberry (page 144), Butterfly Pea Flower (page 147), Carrot (page 150), Cornflower (page 152), Dragon Fruit (page 155)

NOTE

Use the pointy end of a chopstick to gently nudge the dough out of the letter cutter onto a sheet of parchment. These can be baked at 350°F for 5 to 10 minutes and tossed in cinnamon sugar as tiny snacks.

KAPIEDOSCOPE

I cut my competitive teeth on evenings of Scrabble with my bibliophile wordsmith mother. I don't recall much about those matches except that my brother and I never stood a chance against her prowess. Ben and I are more evenly matched, and the competition these days has only heightened. There is always a running game on our coffee table, and sometimes instead of going to bed like responsible adults, we lie awake playing endless rounds on our phones until the loser pouts themselves to sleep.

Occasionally, when I devise one of these alphabet designs, I consider baking the bonus scraps and sneaking them on the board as tiles. S's are usually the most versatile, but sometimes you need those high-point letters like W to nudge your word from wimpy to worthwhile. Whatever your tactic, when it's combined with this bingo of a deeply juicy balsamic grape filling, you're sure to be a winner.

2 disks Beet Pie Dough (page 138)

BALSAMIC GRAPE FILLING

6 cups (2 pounds/907 grams) seedless black grapes, sliced in half

⅔ cup (132 grams) packed light brown sugar

3 tablespoons balsamic vinegar

⅓ cup (38 grams) tapioca starch

1 teaspoon kosher salt

KALEIDOSCOPE DESIGN NEEDS

Parchment paper

½-inch circle cutter

Letter W cutter

Letter V cutter

Paring knife

1. On a floured surface, roll 1 dough disk into a 13-inch circle. Roll the dough onto the rolling pin and unfurl it onto a sheet of parchment paper. Using a ½-inch circle cutter, punch out a hole in the center of the dough.

2. Punch out a ring of seven W's radiating around the center circle.

3. Moving outward, punch a ring of V's in between the W's.

4. Flip the W cutter and cut an offset ring of M's in between the V's.

5. Finish the design with a final outer ring of V's.

6. Slide a flat baking sheet under the parchment and place the perforated pie top in the freezer until frozen solid, about 20 minutes.

7. Roll the second disk of dough into a 14-inch circle. Roll the dough onto the rolling pin and unfurl it over a 9-inch pie pan. Taking the edges of the dough, gently ease the dough into the pan, nestling it into the inner elbows of the pie pan. Trim the excess dough with kitchen shears to create a 1-inch overhang. Fold the overhang back under, creating an elevated edge.

8. To prepare the balsamic grape filling, combine all the ingredients in a large bowl and gently fold with a spatula to coat the fruit.

9. Pour the filling into the pie shell. Use a small pastry brush to lightly dab water around the edge of the dough.

10. Remove the frozen pie top from the freezer, pick it up as one solid piece, and lay it centered on the surface of your filled pie. Let it sit for a few minutes to thaw slightly and settle. Press to seal the edges and run a paring knife around the edge to trim the excess.

recipe continues

11. Chill the entire pie in the freezer while the oven comes to temperature. The pie can be frozen until solid before baking or simply chilled through, about 20 minutes.

12. Preheat the oven to 400°F. Line a rimmed baking sheet with parchment.

13. When the oven comes to temperature, remove the pie from the freezer and place it on the prepared baking sheet.

14. Bake the pie for 25 minutes, then rotate the pie 180 degrees and lower the oven temperature to 350°F. If the edges are already brown, cover with a shield. If the top begins to brown excessively, rest a sheet of foil lightly on top. Continue baking until the filling is bubbling in the center, checking every 30 minutes to rotate the pie and adjust the shields as necessary, 75 to 90 total minutes. (If baking from frozen, add 30 to 45 minutes to the bake time.)

15. Cool the pie completely on a rack before slicing and serving.

SUGGESTED SUBSTITUTIONS

Dough alternatives: Basic (page 134), Black Sesame (page 141), Blueberry (page 144), Butterfly Pea Flower (page 147), Cornflower (page 152), Dragon Fruit (page 155)

Filling alternative: Seedless red grapes

NOTE

Use the pointy end of a chopstick to gently nudge the dough out of the letter cutter onto a sheet of parchment. These can be baked at 350°F for 5 to 10 minutes and tossed in cinnamon sugar.

A GREEN SLATE

My favorite restaurant in the whole world is a meat grill in Honduras. It's called El Patio and the place is configured as a giant version of its namesake, with terra-cotta tiles and outdoor furniture. It's where you go to pack the tabletop with juicy steaks longer than your arm, yucca with crunchy chicharrón, fried plantains with crema, and clay pots full of beans and bubbling cheese heated with hot coals. It's carnivore heaven, and while this pie is no charred churrasco, anything so laden with meat always brings me back to this place and the joys of its feasting scene.

2 disks Spinach Pie Dough (page 162)

TOMATILLO SHORT RIB FILLING

2 pounds (907 grams) boneless beef short ribs, cut into 2-inch pieces

Kosher salt and freshly ground black pepper to taste

¼ cup (59 milliliters) olive oil

1 yellow onion, chopped

4 garlic cloves, peeled and sliced

4 large poblano peppers, seeded and cut into 1-inch pieces

6 carrots, peeled and cut into 1-inch pieces

1 teaspoon ground cumin

1 teaspoon dried oregano, preferably Mexican

1 teaspoon cayenne

1 pound (454 grams) tomatillos, husked and quartered

1. Preheat the oven to 400°F.

2. Season the short ribs liberally with salt and pepper. Seriously, don't be scared!

3. Heat a Dutch oven over medium-high heat and add the oil once hot. Working in batches, brown the short ribs on all sides. Remove them to a plate.

4. Add the onion, garlic, peppers, and carrots and sauté until the onion is translucent, about 10 minutes. Season generously with salt and pepper and add the cumin, oregano, and cayenne. Add the tomatillos and cook until softened, 3 to 5 minutes.

5. Deglaze the pot with the beer and lime juice, scraping up the toasty brown bits on the bottom of the pot, and bring the mixture to a boil. Return the short ribs and the juices on the plate to the pot. Add the bay leaves and make sure the ingredients are mostly submerged in the liquid. Cover the pot securely and transfer to the oven.

6. Braise for 2 hours, until the meat is fork-tender. Season with salt to taste. Cool completely before filling the pie shell.

7. On a floured surface, roll 1 dough disk into a 13 × 15-inch rectangle. Roll the dough onto the rolling pin and unfurl it onto a sheet of parchment paper.

8. Using the ruler and the rolling pastry wheel, cut a 12 × 6-inch rectangle.

9. Cut the remaining dough surrounding the rectangle into approximately ½ × 15-inch strips and set the strips aside.

recipe continues

Two 12-ounce cans (355 milliliters) light beer

Juice of 2 limes

2 bay leaves

Parchment paper

Rolling pastry wheel

Paring knife

Ruler

Dough alternatives: Basic (page 134), Carrot (page 150), Spinach with poppy seeds (page 162), Whole Wheat Cheddar Chive (page 165)

NOTE
The short rib filling can be made 1 or 2 days ahead.

10. Using the pastry wheel or a paring knife, cut consecutively smaller rectangles within the 12 × 6-inch rectangle, alternating between ¼ inch and ½ inch in strip width. Make one final long-edge cut to divide the rectangles in half. I like to make this cut off-center so the halves differ in length for visual variety.

11. Slide a flat baking sheet under the parchment and place the pie top in the freezer until frozen solid, about 20 minutes.

12. Roll the second disk of dough into a 14-inch circle. Roll the dough onto the rolling pin and unfurl it over a 9-inch pie pan. Taking the edges of the dough, gently ease the dough into the pan, nestling it into the inner elbows of the pie pan. Trim the excess dough with kitchen shears to create a 1-inch overhang. Fold the overhang back under, creating an elevated edge.

13. Scoop the short rib filling into the pie shell and smooth with a spatula to create a flat surface.

14. Place the largest ½-inch-thick rectangle cutouts asymmetrically back to back on the surface of the pie, leaving ¼ inch between them. Place the remaining ½-inch rectangle cutouts on the pie, each cutout nesting in the next largest, leaving a ¼-inch space where the ¼-inch cutouts had been.

15. Complete the design by placing dough strips on either side of the center design, leaving ¼-inch space between each strip. Gently press all the strips to secure the edges. Run a paring knife around the edge of the pie to trim the excess.

16. Chill the entire pie in the freezer while the oven comes to temperature.

17. Preheat the oven to 400°F.

18. When the oven comes to temperature, remove the pie from the freezer and place it on a baking sheet. Bake the pie for 25 minutes, then rotate the pie 180 degrees and lower the oven temperature to 350°F. If the edges are already brown, cover with a shield. If the top begins to brown excessively, rest a sheet of foil lightly on top. Continue baking until the top crust is baked through and crisp, checking every 30 minutes to rotate the pie and adjust the shields as necessary, 50 to 75 total minutes. (If baking from frozen, add 30 to 45 minutes to the bake time.)

19. Cool the pie slightly on a rack before slicing and serving.

SQUIGGLE ROOM

Carne asada and cinnamon-dusted pineapple have always been staple items at every family barbecue. I've continued to preach the gospel of grilled pineapple into adulthood, and I'm here to keep spreading the good news. It. Will. Change. Your. Life!

Char the pineapple on the grill for maximum smoky caramelization (griddle inside only if you must), then crown it with a tousle of cherubic curls for a fast track to seventh heaven.

2 disks Basic Pie Dough (page 134)

GRILLED CINNAMON PINEAPPLE FILLING

½ cup (99 grams) granulated sugar

¾ teaspoon ground cinnamon

2 large (4- to 5-pound/ 1.8- to 2.3-kilogram) ripe pineapples

¼ cup (50 grams) packed light brown sugar

¼ cup (28 grams) tapioca starch

1 teaspoon kosher salt

½ tablespoon fresh lime juice

EGG WASH AND SUGAR SPRINKLE

Egg wash (see page 130)

Demerara sugar (optional)

SQUIGGLE DESIGN NEEDS

Parchment paper

Ruler

Rolling pastry wheel

Paring knife

1. Whisk the granulated sugar and cinnamon together in a small bowl. Set aside.

2. Heat a barbecue grill to medium-high. (Alternatively, you can use a cast-iron grill pan or skillet on a stovetop, but turn on your fan!)

3. While the grill heats, prepare the pineapples: Trim off the crown and bottom of a pineapple and cut away the spiky skin. With the pineapple standing upright, slice the fruit into quarters, and cut out the core. Cut each pineapple quarter into 3 long, triangular batons and lay the batons on a rimmed baking sheet. Repeat to cut the other pineapple. Sprinkle all sides of the pineapple with the cinnamon-sugar mixture.

4. Grill the pineapple batons on all sides to char the fruit and caramelize the sugar, 2 to 3 minutes per side. (You *maaaay* want to add an extra pineapple in case you feel compelled to scarf down handfuls of fruit while standing outside, sweet juices running down your arm and all.) Let the pineapple cool to room temperature.

5. Chop the grilled pineapple into 1-inch chunks and toss in a large bowl with the brown sugar, tapioca starch, salt, and lime juice. Set aside.

6. On a floured surface, roll out one dough disk into an 11 × 15-inch rectangle. Roll the dough onto the rolling pin and unfurl it onto a sheet of parchment paper. Using a ruler as a straight edge, cut the rectangle widthwise into ¼-inch strips with a rolling pastry wheel.

7. Slide a flat baking sheet under the parchment and place the dough in the refrigerator to keep cold while proceeding with the design process.

recipe continues

8. Roll out another dough disk into a 13-inch circle. Roll the dough onto the rolling pin and unfurl it over a 9-inch pie pan. Taking the edges of the dough, gently ease the dough into the pan, nestling it into the inner elbows of the pie pan. Trim the excess dough with kitchen shears to create a 1-inch overhang. Fold the overhang back under, creating an elevated edge.

9. Pour the pineapple filling into the pie shell, pressing lightly with a spatula to create a somewhat flat surface.

10. Remove the dough strips from the refrigerator. Stand one strip of dough on its side, and gently scrunch into a squiggly pattern. Slide a paring knife under the squiggled dough and carefully transfer it to the center of the pie. Arrange the next strip of dough in a different squiggle pattern, scoop with a paring knife, and place on the surface of the pie adjacent to the first squiggle.

11. Continue arranging strips of dough in varying squiggle patterns and fitting them together on the pie until the entire surface has been covered. Strips can also be trimmed to fit in the remaining spaces as the design approaches completion.

12. Run a paring knife around the edge of the pie to trim any excess dough. Make sure no squiggly sections are hanging over the edge of the pie, as they will fall off and burn during baking.

13. Chill the entire pie in the freezer while the oven comes to temperature. The pie can be frozen until solid before baking or simply chilled through, about 20 minutes.

14. Preheat the oven to 425°F. Line a rimmed baking sheet with parchment.

15. When the oven has come to temperature, remove the pie from the freezer and place it on the prepared baking sheet. Brush with the egg wash. Sprinkle with demerara sugar, if desired.

16. Bake the pie for 25 minutes, then rotate the pie 180 degrees and lower the oven temperature to 400°F. If the edges are already brown, cover with a shield. Continue baking until the filling is bubbling rapidly in the center, checking every 30 minutes to rotate the pie and adjust the shield, 60 to 90 minutes total.

17. Cool the pie completely on a rack before slicing and serving.

SUGGESTED SUBSTITUTIONS

Dough alternatives: Beet (page 138), Blueberry (page 144), Butterfly Pea Flower (page 147), Cornflower (page 152), Dragon Fruit (page 155)

I take inspiration anywhere my eye catches—from gritty public bathrooms to shirts on unsuspecting passersby to jaunty shadow angles at certain times of the day. I've made pies and tarts modeled after floor tile, storm drains, clumps of tangled foliage, and in this case, a trendy bamboo purse that made the rounds on all the fashion blogs one season.

I rarely carry purses, as I irrationally prefer to cram everything into pockets that are never deep enough. But if I had to choose an everyday bag, it would definitely be a colorful geometric satchel with capacity for pounds of strawberries and mangos in one snug go like this playful pie pouch. With a radiant solar design and punchy colors, your pie will shine like one in a million even after everyone jumps on the trend.

1 disk Carrot Pie Dough (page 150)

2 disks Dragon Fruit Pie Dough (page 155)

STRAWBERRY MANGO PASSION FRUIT FILLING

1 pound (454 grams) strawberries, hulled and cut into ¼-inch slices (about 3 cups)

1¼ pounds (567 grams) mangos, cut into ½-inch chunks (about 3 large mangos)

¼ cup (2 ounces/56 grams) fresh or frozen passion fruit pulp

1 cup (198 grams) granulated sugar

⅓ cup (38 grams) tapioca starch

1 teaspoon kosher salt

1. On a floured surface, roll the disk of carrot pie dough into a 12-inch square. Roll the dough onto the rolling pin and unfurl it onto a sheet of parchment paper. Using a ruler as a straight edge, trim off the rough edges and then cut the square into ⅛-inch strips with a rolling pastry wheel (run the pastry wheel through a small mound of flour if it begins to stick while slicing).

2. Slide a flat baking sheet under the parchment and place the dough in the refrigerator to keep cold while proceeding with the design process.

3. Roll one disk of the dragon fruit dough into a 13-inch circle. Roll the dough onto the rolling pin and unfurl it onto a sheet of parchment paper. Using a 1-inch circle cutter, punch out a hole in the center of the dough.

4. Remove the carrot dough strips from the refrigerator and slide the sheet of parchment onto your work surface. Lightly brush 9 evenly spaced stripes of water on the dragon fruit dough, radiating like spokes around the circle cutout. Place 9 carrot strips where the water has been brushed, lining one end of each strip against the edge of the center circle.

5. Brush a stripe of water in between each carrot strip and place another ring of carrot strips. The ends of this second ring should be offset from the center circle, forming a ring of their own.

recipe continues

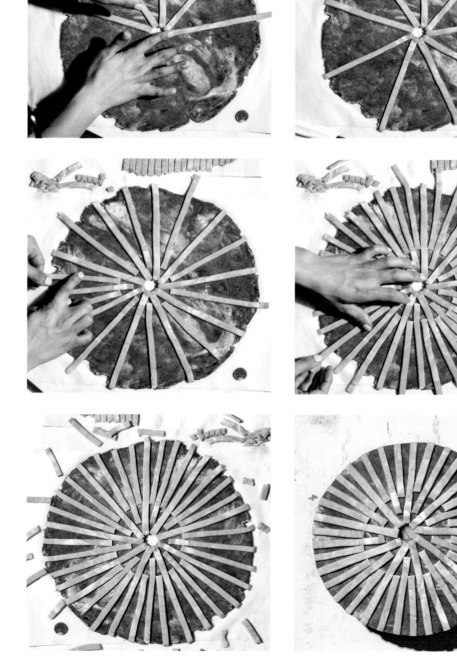

Parchment paper

Ruler

Pastry wheel

1-inch circle cutter

Small bowl of water

Pastry brush

Paring knife

SUGGESTED
SUBSTITUTIONS

Dough alternatives: Basic (page 134), Beet (page 138), Blueberry (page 144), Butterfly Pea Flower (page 147), Cornflower (page 152), Spinach (page 162)

NOTE

You can use small shape cutters to punch out shapes from the extra dough scraps to bake as pie cookies (see page 130) or to use in other pie designs, such as Block and Awe (page 255). The dough can also be gently pressed into a ball (do not knead), wrapped tightly in plastic, and chilled before re-rolling once as marbled dough for a pie like Caught Off Shard (page 264).

6. Place a third and final ring of carrot strips in between each established strip, brushing the dragon fruit dough with water beforehand to secure the strips. Slide a flat baking sheet under the parchment and place the pie top in the freezer until frozen solid, about 20 minutes.

7. Roll the second disk of dragon fruit dough into a 14-inch circle. Roll the dough onto the rolling pin and unfurl it over a 9-inch pie pan. Taking the edges of the dough, gently ease the dough into the pan, nestling it into the inner elbows of the pie pan. Trim the excess dough with kitchen shears to create a 1-inch overhang. Fold the overhang back under, creating an elevated edge.

8. To prepare the strawberry mango passion fruit filling, combine all the ingredients in a large bowl and gently fold with a spatula to coat the fruit in sugar and tapioca starch.

9. Pour the filling into the pie shell. Use a pastry brush to lightly dab water around the edge of the pie.

10. Remove the frozen pie top from the freezer, pick it up as one solid piece, and lay it centered on the surface of your filled pie. Let it sit for a few minutes to thaw slightly and settle. Press to seal the edges, then run a paring knife around the edge to trim the excess.

11. Chill the entire pie in the freezer while the oven comes to temperture. The pie can be frozen until solid before baking or simply chilled through, about 20 minutes.

12. Preheat the oven to 400°F. Line a rimmed baking sheet with parchment.

13. When the oven comes to temperature, remove the pie from the freezer and place on the prepared baking sheet. Bake the pie for 25 minutes, then rotate the pie 180 degrees and lower the oven temperature to 350°F. If the edges are already brown, cover with a shield. If the top begins to brown excessively, rest a sheet of foil lightly on top. Continue baking until the filling is bubbling in the center, checking every 30 minutes to rotate the pie and adjust the shields as necessary, 80 to 100 total minutes. (If baking from frozen, add 30 to 45 minutes to the bake time.)

14. Cool the pie completely on a rack before slicing and serving.

SPOKE SIGNALS

I was deeply unhappy and feeling directionless in my office job when I first spun this pie wheel. I felt trapped in a vortex of monotony but didn't know how to break the cycle. What has become known as my Signature Spoke spiraled out of that season of stasis.

From its unassuming inception in my personal kitchen, it has since been dubbed "the modern lattice" and, against all odds, has made its rounds through restaurants, homes, and media platforms all over the world. Today, it comes full circle as a mainstay of this book. This design now represents my name, my brand, and an entire modern pie movement. I once was lost but now I'm round, and this is a testament that the swirled sometimes works in mysterious ways. So if you're searching for a signal to get rolling, circle this one.

2 disks Basic Pie Dough (page 134)

BLUEBARB FILLING

3 cups (18 ounces/510 grams) fresh or frozen blueberries

3 cups (1 pound/454 grams) fresh or frozen rhubarb, cut into ¼-inch slices

1 cup (198 grams) granulated sugar

⅓ cup (38 grams) tapioca starch

½ tablespoon fresh lime juice

1 teaspoon kosher salt

EGG WASH AND SUGAR SPRINKLE

Egg wash (see page 130)

Demerara sugar (optional)

1. Roll 1 dough disk into an 11 × 15-inch rectangle. Roll the dough onto the rolling pin and unfurl it onto a sheet of parchment paper. Using a ruler as a straight edge and a rolling pastry wheel, cut the rectangle widthwise into at least 30 ¼-inch strips.

2. Slide a flat baking sheet under the parchment and place the dough in the refrigerator to keep cold while proceeding with the pie.

3. Roll the second dough disk into a 14-inch circle. Roll the dough onto the rolling pin and unfurl it over a 9-inch pie pan. Taking the edges of the dough, gently ease the dough into the pan, nestling it into the inner elbows of the pie pan. Trim the excess dough with kitchen shears to create a 1-inch overhang. Fold the overhang back under, creating an elevated edge.

4. To make the bluebarb filling, set aside ¼ cup (43 grams) of the blueberries. Combine the remaining blueberries, rhubarb, sugar, tapioca starch, lime juice, and salt in a large bowl. Gently fold with a spatula until all the fruit pieces are coated.

5. Pour the filling into the pie shell.

6. Place a 2-inch circle cutter in the center of the filling as a reference point. Using a small pastry brush, lightly dab water around the edge of the pie shell.

7. Remove the dough strips from the fridge. Gently pick up a strip of dough, handling it only from the ends, and lay it across

recipe continues

Parchment paper

Ruler

Pastry wheel

2-inch circle cutter

Small bowl of water

Pastry brush

Paring knife

the pie, with the strip grazing the outside of the circle cutter. Lightly press the strip into the edges of the pie to secure.

8. Place another dough strip across the pie. The center of this second strip should lay slightly on top of the first and also graze the center circle cutter. The end of the strip in your left hand should rest ½ inch to the left of the first strip and the end in your right hand to the right of the first.

9. Continue laying dough strips in this fashion, working your way around the pie surface twice. Resist the urge to manually curve each strip. The optical illusion of the full design inspires a curved effect, but the individual strips should be maintained as straight lines.

10. Press the edges of the pie to secure the strips in place. Holding a paring knife at a 45-degree angle to your work surface, run it around the edge of the pie pan to trim the excess dough.

11. Gently remove the center ring cutter and carefully fill the crater with the ¼ cup of reserved blueberries.

12. Chill the entire pie in the freezer until the oven has come to temperature. The pie can be frozen solid or simply chilled through, about 20 minutes.

13. Preheat the oven to 425°F. Line a rimmed baking sheet with parchment and prepare the egg wash.

14. When the oven has reached temperature, remove the pie from the freezer and place it on the prepared baking sheet. Brush with the egg wash and sprinkle with demerara sugar, if desired.

15. Bake the pie for 25 minutes, then rotate the pie 180 degrees and lower the oven temperature to 350°F. If the edges are already brown, cover with a shield. If the top begins to brown excessively, rest a sheet of foil lightly on top. Continue baking until the filling is bubbling in the center, checking every 30 minutes to rotate the pie and adjust the shields as necessary, 80 to 100 total minutes. (If baking from frozen, add 30 to 45 minutes to the bake time.)

16. Cool the pie completely on a rack before slicing and serving.

Dough alternatives: Beet (page 138), Black Sesame (page 141), Blueberry (page 144), Butterfly Pea Flower (page 147), Cornflower (page 152), Dragon Fruit (page 155)

IN IT TO SPIN IT

A reporter once asked me about guilty pleasures from my youth. Nacho cheese of the neon variety is a shameful one, but *Dirty Dancing: Havana Nights* was perhaps my guiltiest. It's a terrible movie with awful writing, but it also contains romantic rooftop dancing sequences, a hip-shaking soundtrack, and a very sheepish Diego Luna.

My bffs and I watched it hundreds (and hundreds) of times, and it ignited a salsa frenzy in us. We took rec classes with sweaty creeps at the gym and, when we mastered the basics, ventured out to the clubs (the most notable of which was called Hot Monkey Love, because of course).

We all know hips don't lie, and mine invariably tell the stiff, robotic truth. But this is pie and this pinwheel design will twist and shout whether you yourself can shake it or not. And, in any case, with supportive partners like tart strawberry rhubarb and nutty sweet pistachio frangipane, you'll definitely be in it to spin it.

2 disks Basic Pie Dough (page 134)

PISTACHIO FRANGIPANE FILLING

½ cup (60 grams) roasted unsalted shelled pistachios

¼ cup (50 grams) granulated sugar

¼ teaspoon kosher salt

4 tablespoons (½ stick/57 grams) unsalted butter, at room temperature, cut into cubes

2 tablespoons (18 grams) all-purpose flour

1 large egg

½ teaspoon pure vanilla extract

STRAWBERRY RHUBARB FILLING

2 pounds (907 grams) fresh strawberries, hulled and cut into ¼-inch slices (about 5½ cups)

1. Roll 1 dough disk into an 11 × 15-inch rectangle. Roll the dough onto the rolling pin and unfurl it onto a sheet of parchment paper. Using a ruler as a straight edge and a rolling pastry wheel, trim off the rough edges, then cut the rectangle crosswise into ¼-inch strips, leaving a 1-inch strip of dough on the side.

2. Using a ¾-inch circle cutter, punch out one dough circle from the remaining 1-inch strip. Slide a flat baking sheet under the parchment and place the dough in the refrigerator to keep cold while proceeding with the pie.

3. Roll the second disk of dough into a 14-inch circle. Roll the dough onto the rolling pin and unfurl it over a 9-inch pie pan. Taking the edges of the dough, gently ease the dough into the pan, nestling it into the inner elbows of the pie pan. Trim the excess dough with kitchen shears to create a 1-inch overhang. Fold the overhang back under, creating an elevated edge. Place the pie shell in the refrigerator to keep cold while preparing the filling.

4. To prepare the pistachio frangipane filling, blitz the pistachios in a food processor until finely ground. Add the sugar and salt and pulse several times to blend.

recipe continues

5 ounces (142 grams) fresh or frozen rhubarb, cut into ¼-inch slices (about 1 cup)

½ cup (99 grams) granulated sugar

¼ cup (28 grams) tapioca starch

½ teaspoon kosher salt

EGG WASH AND SUGAR SPRINKLE

Egg wash (see page 130)

Demerara sugar (optional)

PINWHEEL DESIGN NEEDS

Parchment paper

Ruler

Rolling pastry wheel

¾-inch circle cutter

Small bowl of water

Pastry brush

Paring knife

5. Add the softened butter and process until the mixture begins to come together. Add the flour, egg, and vanilla and process until the mixture is smooth, pausing to scrape down the sides of the food processor with a spatula. Set aside.

6. To prepare the strawberry rhubarb filling, combine all the ingredients in a large bowl and gently fold with a spatula until the fruit is evenly coated.

7. Scoop the pistachio frangipane into the pie shell and smooth it into an even layer with an offset spatula.

8. Pour the strawberry rhubarb filling on top of the frangipane and use a spatula to gently press the fruit down to create a somewhat flat surface.

9. Remove the dough strips from the refrigerator. Place one strip vertically down the center of the pie and gently press into the edges of the pie to secure. Place another strip horizontally across the surface of the pie, perpendicular to the first strip.

10. Place two diagonal strips in the form of an X, dividing each pie quadrant in half. All four strips should intersect at the center point of the pie and divide it visually into 8 wedges.

11. Each one-eighth section of the pie consists of five small straight strips radiating along the center line and secured on the edge of the pie. Lightly brush the vertical center line and the edge of the pie with water.

12. Cut a strip of dough in half, then place one end at the center of the pie and the other end on the edge of the pie ¼ inch from the center-top strip. Press gently to secure. Place another small strip on the vertical center line, ¼ inch above the previously placed strip, and ending on the edge of the pie, ¼ inch to the right of the previous strip. Continue placing three more small strips, moving up the center line and along the edge of the pie. The end of the fifth strip should touch the center marker of the next one-eighth section. Resist the urge to manually curve each strip. The optical illusion of the full design will create a curved effect, but the individual strips should be maintained as straight lines when placed.

13. Repeat this process for each one-eighth section of the pie. (If your dough becomes warm and melty at any point, you can

recipe continues

slide a baking sheet under the parchment and pop the whole operation into the refrigerator for 5 minutes to chill.)

14. Brush a bit of water in the center of the design and place the dough circle in the middle.

15. Gently press around the edge of the pie to secure the strips. Run a paring knife around the edge of the pie to trim the excess dough.

16. Chill the entire pie in the freezer until the oven has come to temperature. The pie can be frozen solid before baking or simply chilled through, about 20 minutes.

17. Preheat the oven to 425°F. Line a rimmed baking sheet with parchment and prepare the egg wash.

18. When the oven has come to temperature, remove the pie from the freezer and place it on the prepared baking sheet. Brush with egg wash and sprinkle with demerara sugar, if desired.

19. Bake the pie for 25 minutes, then rotate the pie 180 degrees and lower the oven temperature to 350°F. If the edges are already brown, cover with a shield. If the top begins to brown excessively, rest a sheet of foil lightly on top. Continue baking until the filling is bubbling in the center, checking every 30 minutes to rotate the pie and adjust the shields as necessary, 80 to 100 total minutes. (If baking from frozen, add 30 to 45 minutes to the bake time.)

20. Cool the pie completely on a rack before slicing and serving.

SUGGESTED SUBSTITUTIONS

Dough alternatives: Beet (page 138), Black Sesame (page 141), Blueberry (page 144), Butterfly Pea Flower (page 147), Cornflower (page 152), Dragon Fruit (page 155)

NOTE

Frangipane is a sweet filling normally made with almonds. Here we use pistachios for a flavor that pairs delightfully with the tartness of the strawberry-rhubarb combination.

ALL STRINGS CONSIDERED

The first iteration of this design was a complete accident. It was the failed result of an entirely different plan. Still, I reluctantly posted it to Instagram after another pie-dea fell through. As luck would have it, Design Milk, an online magazine dedicated to modern design, shared the photo with their vast audience, immediately catapulting it into Internet notoriety. My Lokokitchen Instagram account had been slowly building momentum, but less than two months after its genesis, this was the catalyst that pushed the doughball down the hill. And what a wild ride it's been.

The apple and gingerbread caramel combination has been a crowd favorite, and one I lean on no matter the season. Year-end celebrations, Christmas in July, or general craving for pie . . . this warmly spiced twist on the American classic is one to be considered seriously.

2 disks Blueberry Pie Dough (page 144)

APPLE WITH GINGERBREAD CARAMEL FILLING

3½ pounds (1.6 kilograms) apples, such as Gala or Honeycrisp (6 to 8 large apples)

½ cup (99 grams) granulated sugar

¼ cup (28 grams) tapioca starch

1 teaspoon kosher salt

1 cup gingerbread caramel (see page 109), cold or at room temperature, plus extra for drizzling (optional)

1. On a floured surface, roll 1 dough disk into an 11 × 15-inch rectangle. Roll the dough onto the rolling pin and unfurl it onto a sheet of parchment paper. Using a ruler as a straight edge and a rolling pastry wheel, cut the rectangle crosswise into ¼-inch strips (you will need about 30). Slide a flat baking sheet under the parchment and place the dough in the refrigerator to keep cold while proceeding with the pie.

2. Roll the second disk of dough into a 14-inch circle. Roll the dough onto the rolling pin and unfurl it over a 9-inch pie pan. Taking the edges of the dough, gently ease the dough into the pan, nestling it into the inner elbows of the pie pan. Trim the excess dough with kitchen shears to create a 1-inch overhang. Fold the overhang back under, creating an elevated edge.

3. Peel, core, and cut the apples into ¼-inch slices. Toss them in a large bowl with the sugar, tapioca starch, and salt.

4. Fill the pie shell with two layers of apples slices fitted closely together. Place a few more layers of slices around the edges, going three-quarters of the way up the pie shell sides, leaving a well in the center.

5. Pour the cooled gingerbread caramel into the well.

6. Fill the pie shell with the remaining apple slices, doming the fruit slightly in the center.

recipe continues

PIE DESIGNS

Parchment paper

Ruler

Pastry wheel

2-inch circle cutter

Small bowl of water

Pastry brush

Paring knife

**Dough alternatives:
Basic (page 134), Beet
(page 138), Black Sesame
(page 141), Butterfly
Pea Flower (page 147),
Cornflower (page 152),
Dragon Fruit (page 155)**

NOTE

The gingerbread caramel
can be made days in
advance and stored in
the refrigerator until use.

7. Place a 2-inch circle cutter slightly left of center on the pie surface. Using a pastry brush, lightly brush water around the edge of the pie to make it easier to adhere the strips.

8. Remove the dough strips from the refrigerator. Lay one strip of dough vertically down the center of the pie to the right of the circle cutter and gently press the strip into the edges to secure.

9. Continue laying strips across the surface of the pie with the ends ½ inch apart, and radiating around the circle cutter.

10. The last strip placed will end in the same spot as the first placed strip began, culminating in a teardrop cavity. (If your dough becomes warm and melty at any point, you can slide a baking sheet under the parchment and pop the whole operation into the refrigerator for 5 minutes to chill.)

11. Place five vertical strips spaced ½ inch apart to the right of the very first strip.

12. Place five horizontal strips below the circle cutter, spaced ½ inch apart. Press the edges of the pie to secure the strips.

13. Holding a paring knife at a 45-degree angle to your work surface, run it around the edge of the pie pan to trim the excess dough. Gently remove the center ring cutter.

14. Chill the entire pie in the freezer until the oven has come to temperature. The pie can be frozen solid before baking or simply chilled through, about 20 minutes.

15. Preheat the oven to 400°F and line a rimmed baking sheet with parchment.

16. When the oven has come to temperature, remove the pie from the freezer and place it on the prepared baking sheet.

17. Bake the pie for 25 minutes, then rotate the pie 180 degrees and lower the oven temperature to 350°F. If the edges are already brown, cover with a shield. If the top begins to brown excessively, rest a sheet of foil lightly on top. Continue baking until the filling is bubbling in the center, checking every 30 minutes to rotate the pie and adjust the shields as necessary, 80 to 100 total minutes. (If baking from frozen, add 30 to 45 minutes to the bake time.)

18. If you're feeling especially saucy, drizzle extra caramel into the center cavity while the pie is still steamy hot. Cool the pie completely on a rack before slicing and serving.

I spent a stupidly privileged month in the southern city of Cádiz preceding my year of study in Barcelona, and it was a vision out of a Hemingway novel. I spent every night in open-air plazas sipping spiced sangrias and tinto de veranos (red wine with lemon Fanta on ice), and I ache with gratitude whenever I reflect on that ridiculous season in life. What even. Many of my pies are swathed in nostalgia, and this one is no different. Salud to balmy nights, the gift of experiences we hardly deserve, and the sweets, like this pie, that result when we stir those memories.

2 disks Dragon Fruit Pie Dough (page 155)

SANGRIA JAM FILLING

1 pound (454 grams) strawberries, hulled and cut into ¼-inch slices (about 2¾ cups)

2 cups (11 ounces/312 grams) fresh or frozen blackberries

1 cup (198 grams) granulated sugar

¼ cup (28 grams) tapioca starch

½ cup (118 milliliters) fruity red wine, such as merlot or Beaujolais

½ cup (118 milliliters) fresh orange juice (from about 2 large oranges)

Zest of 1 orange

1 teaspoon kosher salt

½ teaspoon ground cinnamon

2½ cups (1 pound/454 grams) fresh or frozen red cherries, pitted

1. To prepare the sangria jam filling, combine the strawberries, blackberries, sugar, tapioca starch, red wine, orange juice, orange zest, salt, and cinnamon together in a medium pot. Cook over medium heat until thickened, stirring with a spatula, 12 to 15 minutes. Fold in the cherries and allow the mixture to cool to room temperature.

2. Roll 1 dough disk into an 11 × 15-inch rectangle. Roll the dough onto the rolling pin and unfurl it onto a sheet of parchment paper. Using a ruler as a straight edge, cut the rectangle widthwise into ¼-inch strips with a rolling pastry wheel. Slide a flat baking sheet under the parchment and place the dough in the refrigerator to keep cold while proceeding with the pie.

3. Roll the second disk of dough into a 14-inch circle. Roll the dough onto the rolling pin and unfurl it over a 9-inch pie pan. Taking the edges of the dough, gently ease the dough into the tin, nestling it into the inner elbows of the pie pan. Trim the excess dough with kitchen shears to create a 1-inch overhang. Fold the overhang back under, creating an elevated edge.

4. Fill the pie shell with the cooled fruit jam. Using a pastry brush, lightly brush water around the edge of the pie to make it easier to adhere the strips.

5. Remove the dough strips from the refrigerator. Lay one strip of dough vertically down the center of the pie and gently press the strip into the edges to secure.

6. Place a 2-inch circle cutter to the left of the strip and above center, touching the strip.

recipe continues

DOUBLE SHELL DESIGN NEEDS

Parchment paper

Ruler

Pastry wheel

2-inch circle cutter

Small bowl of water

Pastry brush

Paring knife

7. Continue laying strips across the surface of the pie, with the ends ½ inch apart, radiating around the circle cutter. Make sure the strips graze the center circle cutter until you reach its left edge. At this point, the last few strips placed will not touch the circle cutter but will continue down the edge of the pie, culminating in a shell-like string structure and a teardrop cavity. The last strip will end in the same spot as the very first strip. (If your dough becomes warm and melty at any point, you can slide a baking sheet under the parchment and pop the whole operation into the refrigerator for 5 minutes to chill.)

8. Remove the circle cutter and lay a strip down the center of the pie lined up with the very first strip placed. Gently rest the circle cutter to the right of this strip and below center. Repeat the process of laying strips across the surface of the pie, with the ends ½ inch apart, radiating around the circle cutter. This arrangement should be the mirror image of the first shell half of strips placed. Gently remove the circle cutter.

9. Press the edges of the pie to secure the strips. Holding a paring knife at a 45-degree angle to your work surface, run it around the edge of the pie pan to trim the excess dough.

10. Chill the entire pie in the freezer until the oven has come to temperature. The pie can be frozen solid before baking or simply chilled through, about 20 minutes.

11. Preheat the oven to 400°F and line a rimmed baking sheet with parchment.

12. When the oven has come to temperature, remove the pie from the freezer and place it on the prepared baking sheet.

13. Bake the pie for 25 minutes, then rotate the pie 180 degrees and lower the oven temperature to 350°F. If the edges are already brown, cover with a shield. Since the dragon fruit color can be delicate, lightly covering the top of the pie with foil is recommended at this point in order to preserve the vibrancy of the color. Remove the foil for the last 10 to 15 minutes of baking to allow the top crust to cook through. Since this filling is precooked, bake until the crust is crisp and the filling is bubbling around the edges, checking every 30 minutes to rotate the pie and adjust the shield as necessary, 60 to 85 total minutes. (If baking from frozen, add 30 to 45 minutes to the bake time.)

14. Cool the pie completely on a rack before slicing and serving.

SUGGESTED SUBSTITUTIONS

Dough alternatives: Basic (page 134), Beet (page 138), Black Sesame (page 141), Blueberry (page 144), Butterfly Pea Flower (page 147), Cornflower (page 152)

LATTICE QUO

I was sitting at a lunch table outside, waiting for the bell to announce the start of the school day. In San Diego, days often start overcast and eventually give way to scorching temperatures as the marine layer dissipates. I was clad in the standard Southern Californian uniform of shorts and a tank top and was feeling the morning chill. I pulled a blue sweatshirt out of my backpack, drew my knees up, stretched the cotton taut over my legs, and then tucked my arms in, too. Some kids ran by, jostling the table, and I felt myself teetering from the impact. The sweatshirt was too tight for my limbs to beat a hasty retreat, and soon I was plummeting to the concrete, face first.

This almond-scented apricot and honey pairing is face-smashingly good, minus the blood, purple lip, and elementary school trauma. Skip the teal cocoon and keep warm with this pie instead.

2 disks Cornflower Pie Dough (page 152)

HONEY ALMOND APRICOT FILLING

3 pounds (1.4 kilograms) ripe apricots, unpeeled, pitted and cut into ½-inch slices (about 25 apricots)

½ cup (170 grams) honey

½ cup (99 grams) granulated sugar

⅓ cup (38 grams) tapioca starch

1 teaspoon kosher salt

1 teaspoon almond extract

EGG WASH AND SUGAR SPRINKLE

Egg wash (see page 130)

Demerara sugar (optional)

1. Roll 1 dough disk into an 11 × 15-inch rectangle. Roll the dough onto the rolling pin and unfurl it onto a sheet of parchment paper. Using a ruler as a straight edge and a rolling pastry wheel, cut the rectangle crosswise into a variety of strips ranging in width from ¼ inch to 2 inches. Slide a flat baking sheet under the parchment and place the dough in the refrigerator to keep cold while proceeding with the pie.

2. Roll the second disk of dough into a 14-inch circle. Roll the dough onto the rolling pin and unfurl it over a 9-inch pie pan. Taking the edges of the dough, gently ease the dough into the pan, nestling it into the inner elbows of the pie pan. Trim the excess dough with kitchen shears to create a 1-inch overhang. Fold the overhang back under, creating an elevated edge.

3. To prepare the honey almond apricot filling, combine all the ingredients in a large bowl and gently fold to coat the fruit. Pour the filling into the prepared pie shell.

4. Remove the chilled dough from the refrigerator. Lay strips of varying width ⅛ inch apart diagonally across the surface of the pie.

5. Starting from the left, fold every other strip of dough back halfway. Lay a strip of dough at a perpendicular diagonal and unfold all the strips.

recipe continues

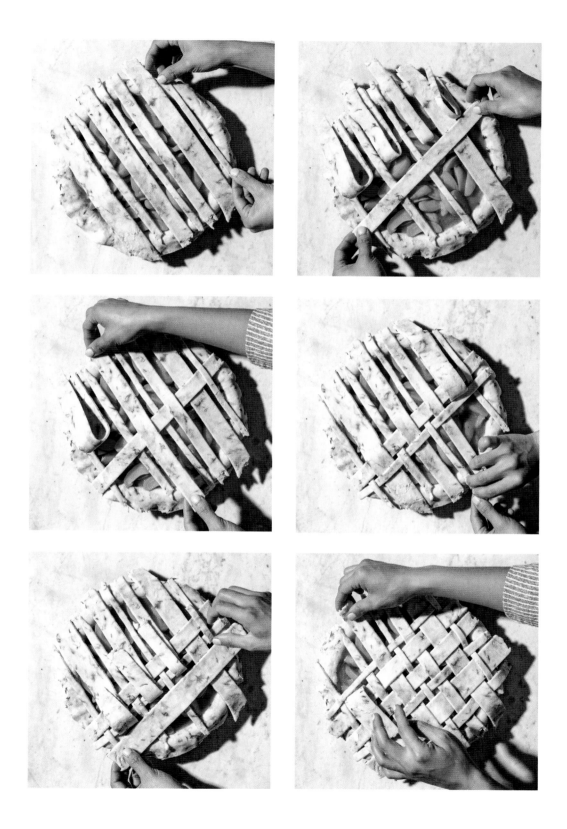

PLAID LATTICE DESIGN NEEDS

Parchment paper

Ruler

Rolling pastry wheel

Paring knife

6. Fold back the previously unfolded strips and lay another cornflower strip. Unfold all the strips. Continue this process to complete a fully woven surface.

7. Use kitchen shears to trim the top and bottom doughs to leave a 1-inch overhang around the edge. Press to seal the strips into the bottom pie shell, and then roll the edges in. Crimp the pie all the way around.

8. Chill the entire pie in the freezer until the oven has come to temperature. The pie can be frozen solid before baking or simply chilled through, about 20 minutes.

9. Preheat the oven to 425°F. Line a rimmed baking sheet with parchment paper and prepare the egg wash.

10. When the oven has come to temperature, place the chilled pie on the prepared baking sheet. Brush the dough strips with egg wash and sprinkle with demerara sugar, if desired.

11. Bake for 25 minutes, then rotate the pie 180 degrees and lower the oven temperature to 400°F. If the edges are already brown, cover with a shield. If the top begins to brown excessively, rest a sheet of foil lightly on top. Continue baking until the filling is bubbling in the center, checking every 30 minutes to rotate the pie and adjust the shields as necessary, 80 to 100 total minutes. (If baking from frozen, add 30 to 45 minutes to the bake time.)

12. Cool the pie completely on a rack before slicing and serving.

SUGGESTED SUBSTITUTIONS

Dough alternatives: Basic (page 134), Beet (page 138), Black Sesame (page 141), Blueberry (page 144), Butterfly Pea Flower (page 147), Dragon Fruit (page 155)

NO ZIG DEAL

At the ripe old age of three, I decided I'd had enough. I rolled up my ultra-soft bunny blanket, packed a snack in my lunchbox, and demanded that my mom hold my hand while I marched around the block. Later that evening, when my dad returned from work and asked about my day, I matter-of-factly told him I had run away from home. "It's no big deal. I might do it again tomorrow."

This simple but pronounced lattice weave requires about the same nonchalant level of commitment. It demands very little, and in the time it takes you to make it once around the block, you'll have a pie ready to bake for the next adventure.

1 disk Butterfly Pea Flower Pie Dough (page 147)

2 disks Cornflower Pie Dough (page 152)

APPLE BERRY FILLING

1½ pounds (680 grams) apples, such as Gala or Honeycrisp (3 or 4 large apples)

1 cup (6 ounces/170 grams) fresh or frozen blueberries

1 cup (6 ounces/170 grams) fresh or frozen blackberries

⅔ cup (132 grams) packed light brown sugar

¼ cup (28 grams) tapioca starch

1 tablespoon fresh lemon juice

1 teaspoon kosher salt

EGG WASH AND SUGAR SPRINKLE

Egg wash (see page 130; optional)

Demerara sugar (optional)

1. On a floured surface, roll the disk of butterfly pea flower dough into an 11 × 15-inch rectangle. Roll the dough onto the rolling pin and unfurl it onto a sheet of parchment paper. Using a ruler as a straight edge and a rolling pastry wheel, cut the rectangle into 12 strips, ¼ inch wide. Reserve the surplus dough for another pie or baking into pie cookies (see page 130). Slide a flat baking sheet under the parchment and place the strips in the refrigerator to keep cold while proceeding with the design process.

2. Roll 1 cornflower dough disk into an 11 × 15-inch rectangle. Roll the dough onto the rolling pin and unfurl it onto a sheet of parchment paper. Using the ruler as a straight edge and the rolling pastry wheel, cut the rectangle into at least 13 strips, 1 inch wide. Gently slide the sheet of parchment on top of the sheet of butterfly pea flower dough strips and return the baking sheet to the refrigerator to chill for at least 5 minutes before proceeding.

3. Remove the chilled dough strips from the refrigerator. On a sheet of parchment, lay 13 vertical strips of dough, alternating between cornflower and butterfly pea flower, leaving no space between the strips.

4. Starting from the left, fold back every two strips of dough, working in pairs of white and blue.

5. Lay a pair of one cornflower and one butterfly pea flower strip perpendicular to the vertical strips and unfold the folded pairs of strips.

recipe continues

PIE DESIGNS

223

Parchment paper

Ruler

Rolling pastry wheel

Paring knife

6. Fold back the previously unfolded vertical strips and lay another pair of cornflower and butterfly pea flower strips, fitting them tightly against the first horizontal pair. Unfold all the vertical strips. (If your dough becomes warm and melty at any point, you can slide a baking sheet under the parchment and pop the whole operation into the refrigerator for 5 minutes to chill.)

7. Continue this process to complete a fully woven surface, adding horizontal strips to the bottom and then to the top.

8. Slide a flat baking sheet under the parchment and freeze the pie top for at least 30 minutes or until it can be easily lifted as one piece. Once the pie top has frozen solid, it can be wrapped well and used to top a pie at a later time. A well-sealed pie top will keep in the freezer for up to 3 months. Handle frozen pie tops gently, as they can shatter.

9. Roll the second disk of cornflower dough into a 14-inch circle. Roll the dough onto the rolling pin and unfurl it over a 9-inch pie pan. Taking the edges of the dough, gently ease the dough into the pan, nestling it into the inner elbows of the pie pan. Trim the excess dough with kitchen shears to create a 1-inch overhang. Fold the overhang back under, creating an elevated edge.

10. To prepare the apple berry filling, peel, core, and chop the apples into ½-inch cubes. Combine the apples and all the remaining ingredients in a large bowl and gently fold with a spatula to coat the fruit.

11. Pour the filling into the prepared pie shell, doming the fruit slightly in the center. Use a pastry brush to lightly dab water around the edge of the pie.

12. Remove the frozen pie top from the freezer and lay on the surface of the filled pie. Allow to sit for a few minutes to thaw slightly and settle. Press the edge of the pie to seal the strips, and run a paring knife around the edge to trim the excess dough.

13. Chill the entire pie in the freezer until the oven has come to temperature. The pie can be frozen solid before baking or simply chilled through, about 20 minutes.

recipe continues

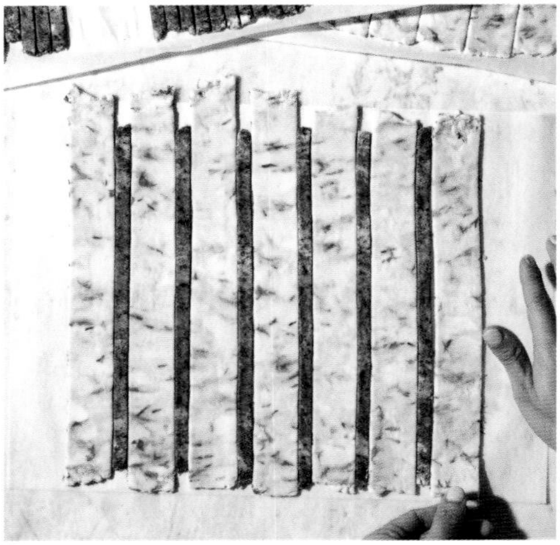

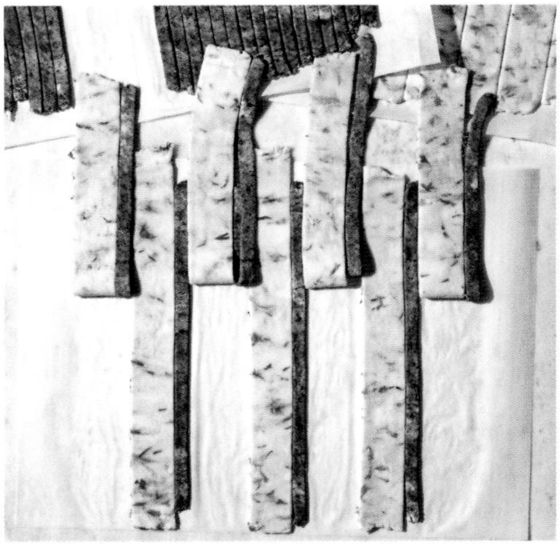

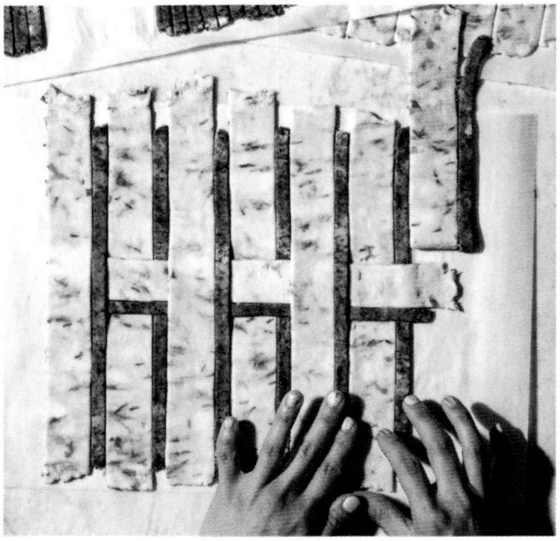

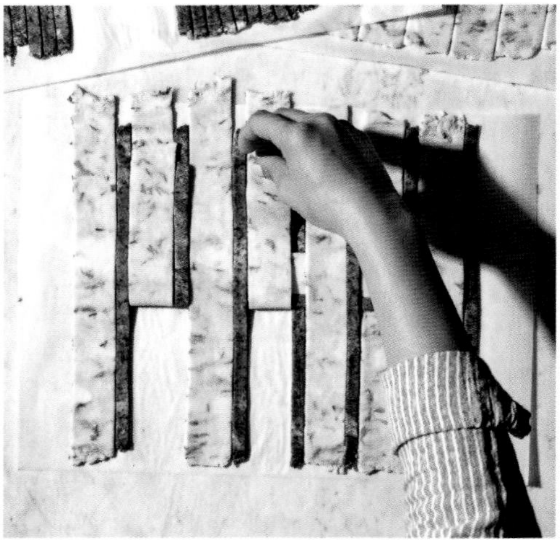

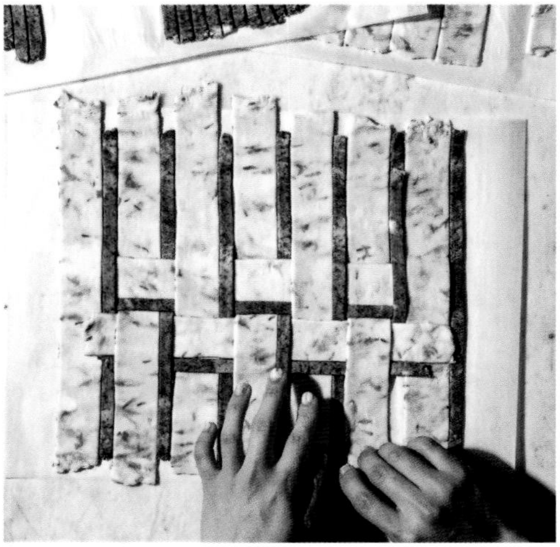

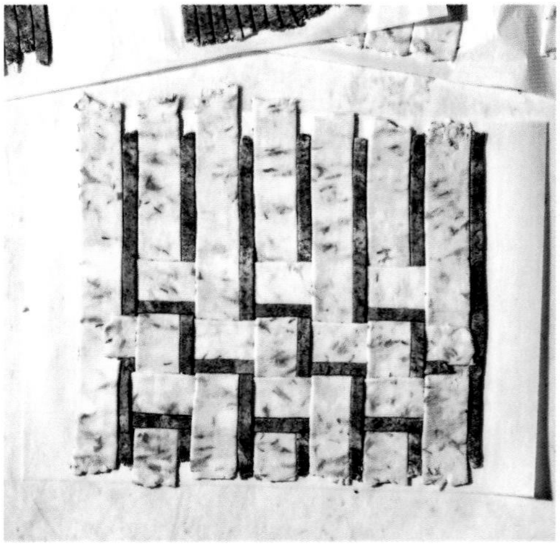

14. Preheat the oven to 400°F. Line a rimmed baking sheet with parchment paper.

15. When the oven has come to temperature, place the chilled pie on the prepared baking sheet. If desired, brush the cornflower dough strips with egg wash and sprinkle with demerara sugar, if desired.

16. Bake for 25 minutes, then rotate the pie 180 degrees and lower the oven temperature to 350°F. If the edges are already brown, cover with a shield. Continue baking until the filling is bubbling rapidly and the top crust looks baked through in the center, checking every 30 minutes to rotate the pie and cover lightly with foil as necessary, 80 to 100 total minutes. (If baking from frozen, add 30 to 45 minutes to the bake time.)

17. Cool the pie completely on a rack before slicing and serving.

SUGGESTED SUBSTITUTIONS

Dough alternatives: Basic (page 134), Beet (page 138), Black Sesame (page 141), Blueberry (page 144), Dragon Fruit (page 155)

NOTE
The trimmed dough scraps can be baked as beautiful woven pie cookies (page 130) or gently pressed into a disk, wrapped, chilled, and re-rolled once more into marbled dough for a pie like Caught Off Shard (page 264).

STRIPE FOR THE PICKING

I have always been a greedy reader. My childhood revolved around weekly visits to the library, maxing out the checkout limit, finishing the stack before the week was up, and then rereading my own stash of favorite books over and over until they fell apart. I was lucky enough to have shelves stuffed with volumes by Laura Ingalls Wilder, Madeleine L'Engle, and Lois Lowry. Novels like *Black Beauty* and *Harriet the Spy* were practically memorized, but among all these beloved books, none were more venerated and repeated than the works of Roald Dahl. *Matilda* and *Danny, the Champion of the World* were unequivocally my favorites, but *James and the Giant Peach* was one story I could not get out of my head. I was never sure if it delighted me or just haunted me, but I still can't see a peach without recalling all of James's tenuous moments in the fruit both on land and at sea.

If I had to revisit a third-grade book report assignment—the kind where you write a few pages of reflection and produce a representative 3-D illustration—this pie, with its unconventional peach filling and blue/green schematic, would be my submission.

2 disks Butterfly Pea Flower Pie Dough (page 144)

1 disk Spinach Pie Dough (page 162)

PEACH MINT FILLING

3 pounds (1.4 kilograms) ripe peaches, pitted and cut into 1-inch chunks (about 7 cups)

⅓ cup (38 grams) tapioca starch

10 to 15 (0.1 ounce/3 grams) fresh mint leaves

1 cup (198 grams) granulated sugar

1 teaspoon kosher salt

Zest of 1 lemon

1. On a floured surface, roll 1 butterfly pea flower dough disk into a 13-inch square. Roll the dough onto the rolling pin and unfurl it onto a sheet of parchment paper. Using a ruler as a straight edge and a rolling pastry wheel, cut the square into ¾-inch strips. Slide a flat baking sheet under the parchment and place the dough in the refrigerator to keep cold while proceeding with the design process.

2. Roll the disk of spinach dough into a 13-inch square. Roll the dough onto the rolling pin and unfurl it onto a sheet of parchment paper. Using a ruler as a straight edge and a rolling pastry wheel, cut the square into ¼-inch strips. Gently slide the parchment on top of the butterfly pea flower strips and return to the refrigerator to chill for at least 5 minutes before proceeding.

3. Remove the chilled strips from the refrigerator and lay the sheet of spinach strips so that the strips are horizontal. Starting from the bottom, fold half the spinach strips in half to the right. Lay a perpendicular butterfly pea flower strip down the middle, then unfold the topmost folded spinach strip over it.

4. Lay another blue strip to the left of the first butterfly pea flower strip and unfold the next spinach strip.

recipe continues

Parchment paper

Baking sheets

Ruler

Rolling pastry wheel

Paring knife

5. Continue in this fashion until you have placed 5 total blue strips. Unfold the remaining folded spinach strips. (If your dough becomes warm and melty at any point, you can slide a baking sheet under the parchment and pop the whole operation into the refrigerator for 5 minutes to chill.)

6. Fold the top half portion of spinach strips to the left. Lay a perpendicular butterfly pea flower strip and unfold the bottommost folded spinach strip.

7. Lay another blue strip to the right of the first butterfly pea flower strip and unfold the next spinach strip.

8. Continue in this fashion until you have placed 5 total blue strips.

9. Unfold the remaining folded spinach strips. Slide a flat baking sheet under the parchment and freeze the pie top for at least 30 minutes or until it can be easily lifted as one piece. Once the pie top has frozen solid, it can be wrapped well and used to top a pie at a later time. A well-sealed pie top will keep in the freezer for up to 3 months. Handle frozen pie tops gently, as they can shatter.

10. Roll the second disk of butterfly pea flower dough into a 14-inch circle. Roll the dough onto the rolling pin and unfurl it over a 9-inch pie pan. Taking the edges of the dough, gently ease the dough into the pan, nestling it into the inner elbows of the pie pan. Trim the excess dough with kitchen shears to create a 1-inch overhang. Fold the overhang back under, creating an elevated edge.

11. To prepare the peach filling, put the peaches and tapioca starch in a large bowl. Set aside.

12. Put the mint leaves, sugar, salt, and lemon zest in a food processor and pulse to blend. Pour the mint sugar into the mixing bowl with the peaches. Gently fold with a spatula to coat the fruit.

13. Scoop the filling into the prepared pie shell, doming the fruit slightly in the center. Use a pastry brush to lightly dab water around the edge of the pie.

14. Remove the frozen pie top from the freezer and lay on the surface of the filled pie. Allow to sit for a few minutes to thaw

recipe continues

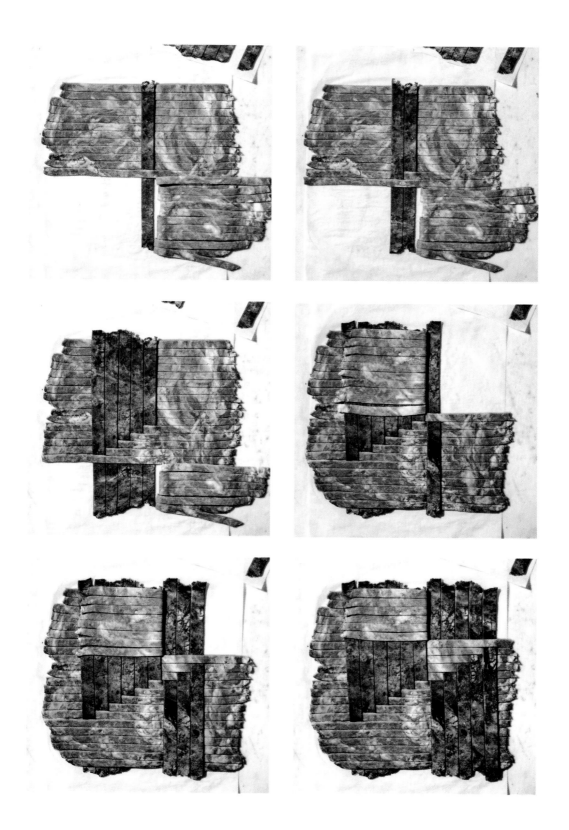

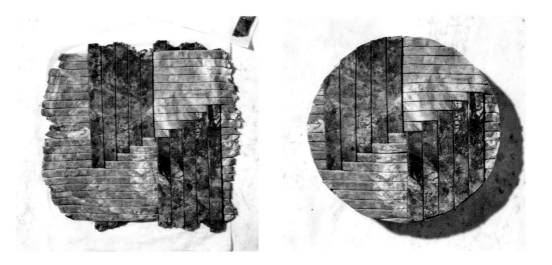

NOTE
The trimmed dough scraps can be baked as beautiful woven pie cookies (see page 130), or gently pressed into a disk, wrapped, chilled, and re-rolled once more into marbled dough for a pie like Caught Off Shard (page 264).

slightly and settle. Press to seal the edges and run a paring knife around the edge to trim the excess dough.

15. Chill the entire pie in the freezer until the oven has come to temperature. The pie can be frozen solid before baking or simply chilled through, about 20 minutes.

16. Preheat the oven to 400°F. Line a rimmed baking sheet with parchment paper.

17. When the oven has come to temperature, place the chilled pie on the prepared baking sheet. Bake for 25 minutes, then rotate the pie 180 degrees and lower the oven temperature to 350°F. If the edges are already brown, cover with a shield. Continue baking until the filling is bubbling rapidly and the top crust looks baked through in the center, checking every 30 minutes to rotate the pie and cover lightly with foil as necessary, 80 to 100 total minutes. (If baking from frozen, add 30 to 45 minutes to the bake time.)

18. Cool the pie completely on a rack before slicing and serving.

SUGGESTED SUBSTITUTIONS

Dough alternatives: Basic (page 134), Beet (page 138), Black Sesame (page 141), Blueberry (page 144), Cornflower (page 152), Dragon Fruit (page 155)

While I was blessed with genes for good hair, height didn't come with the package, so using public transit during rush hour generally means my face is crushed against someone else's armpit while I strain to clutch the overhead handles for dear life. Imagine my delight when I boarded the train one evening and there were open seats everywhere! My one-hour commute was splendidly peaceful and then . . . eerily silent. Only then did I realize that the train had stopped, no one else was around, and it was dark out. After I frantically pushed the "open" button on the doors to no avail and banged on the windows for a few minutes, the conductor walked by and thankfully released me. In my haste, I had taken the wrong metro and completely missed the last stop. I'd narrowly avoided being trapped overnight on a train, and I swore I'd never be caught unawares again. Ten minutes later, I had to flag down a taxi to get home because I'd lost my metro card on the train. Choo choo, hot mess coming through!

Everyone has a tendency to get distracted once in a while, not unlike a certain someone we know, ahem. This design couldn't be better suited to the occasional scatterbrain. The weaving pattern is a simple "every other," and with a quick few scoops of fruit, you'll be on the fast track to success no matter where your mind has wandered.

1 disk Basic Pie Dough (page 134)

2 disks Beet Pie Dough (page 138)

GINGER PEACH MANGO FILLING

3 cups ½-inch-diced fresh ripe mango (about 1 pound/454 grams)

1½ pounds (680 grams) ripe peaches, peeled, pitted, and cut into 1-inch chunks (about 3½ cups)

1 cup (198 grams) granulated sugar

¼ cup (28 grams) tapioca starch

1 teaspoon ground ginger

1 teaspoon kosher salt

1 tablespoon fresh lime juice

1. On a floured surface, roll the disk of basic dough into a 12 × 14-inch rectangle. Roll the dough onto the rolling pin and unfurl it onto a sheet of parchment paper. Using a ruler as a straight edge and a rolling pastry wheel, cut the rectangle widthwise into ¼-inch strips. Slide a flat baking sheet under the parchment and place the dough in the refrigerator to keep cold while proceeding with the design process.

2. Roll 1 disk of beet dough into a 13-inch square. Roll the dough onto the rolling pin and unfurl it onto a sheet of parchment paper. Using a ruler as a straight edge and a rolling pastry wheel, cut the square into ¼-inch strips. Slide a flat baking sheet under the parchment and place the dough in the refrigerator for at least 10 minutes to chill before proceeding.

3. Lay a sheet of parchment paper on your work surface and remove the dough strips from the refrigerator. Place 3 vertical white strips side by side on the sheet of parchment paper. Then place 3 beet dough strips. Alternate between white and magenta sections, laying down 3 strips at a time, until you have four white columns and three magenta columns.

recipe continues

**CHAINLINK WEAVE DESIGN
NEEDS**

Parchment paper

Ruler

Rolling pastry wheel

Paring knife

4. Starting from the left, gently fold back the first white strip. Continue folding back every other strip.

5. Lay a perpendicular white strip across the center and unfold all the vertical strips.

6. Fold back all the previously unfolded vertical strips and lay down a magenta strip, nestling it as close to the horizontal white strip as possible. Unfold all the vertical strips.

7. Continue folding back every other strip, and laying horizontal strips, alternating between white and magenta, until you come to the end of the vertical strips.

8. Rotate the parchment paper 180 degrees and continue the process of folding back vertical strips and laying horizontal strips, alternating colors. (If your dough becomes warm and melty at any point, you can slide a baking sheet under the parchment and pop the whole operation into the refrigerator for 5 minutes to chill.)

9. Once you've completed the full weave, slide a flat baking sheet under the parchment and freeze the pie top for at least 30 minutes or until it can be easily lifted as one piece. Once the pie top has frozen solid, it can be wrapped well and used to top a pie at a later time. A well-sealed pie top will keep in the freezer for up to 3 months. Handle frozen pie tops gently, as they can shatter.

10. While the weave freezes, roll the remaining disk of beet dough into a 14-inch circle. Roll the dough onto the rolling pin and unfurl it over a 9-inch pie pan. Taking the edges of the dough, gently ease the dough into the pan, nestling it into the inner elbows of the pie pan. Trim the excess dough with kitchen shears to create a 1-inch overhang. Fold the overhang back under, creating an elevated edge.

11. To prepare the ginger peach mango filling, combine all the ingredients in a large bowl and gently fold with a spatula to coat the fruit.

12. Pour the filling into the pie shell. Use a pastry brush to lightly brush water around the edge of the pie.

13. Remove the frozen weave from the freezer, pick it up as one solid piece, and lay it centered on the surface of your

recipe continues

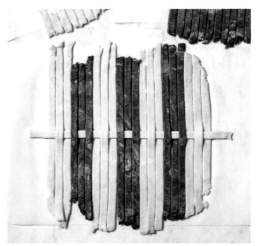

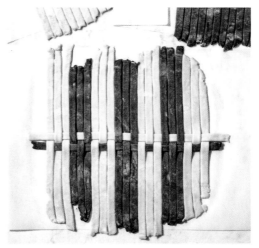

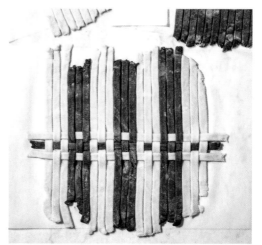

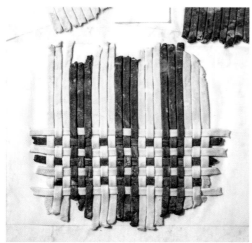

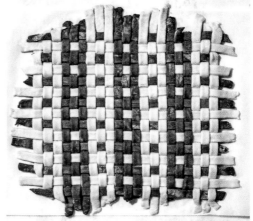

filled pie. Let it sit for a few minutes to thaw slightly and settle. Press to seal the edges, and run a paring knife around the edge to trim the excess dough.

14. Chill the entire pie in the freezer until the oven has come to temperature. The pie can be frozen solid before baking or simply chilled through, about 20 minutes.

15. Preheat the oven to 400°F. Line a rimmed baking sheet with parchment paper.

16. When the oven has come to temperature, place the chilled pie on the prepared baking sheet. Bake for 25 minutes, then rotate the pie 180 degrees and lower the oven temperature to 350°F. If the edges are already brown, cover with a shield. Continue baking until the filling is bubbling rapidly and the top crust looks baked through in the center, checking every 30 minutes to rotate the pie and cover lightly with foil as necessary, 80 to 100 total minutes. (If baking from frozen, add 30 to 45 minutes to the bake time.)

17. Cool the pie completely on a rack before slicing and serving.

SUGGESTED SUBSTITUTIONS

Dough alternatives: Black Sesame (page 141), Blueberry (page 144), Butterfly Pea Flower (page 147), Cornflower (page 152), Dragon Fruit (page 155)

NOTE
The trimmed dough scraps can be baked as beautiful woven pie cookies (see page 130), or gently pressed into a disk, wrapped, chilled, and re-rolled once more into marbled dough for a pie like Caught Off Shard (page 264).

During my first year of living in Paraguay, I took a trip to the arid Chaco desert over Thanksgiving. I spent a few nights in a hotel that was less amenable lodging and more musty Indiana Jones cave. When I went to bed the first night, I kept hearing a syncopated *pak! pak! pak pak!* and, to my horror, discovered legions of hard-shelled insects dropping from the ceiling. I switched on the lights to find the walls covered in trillions of black termites. The entire room was swarming—bugs streaming from the closet, skittering through the floor crevices, pouring out from under the bed, and even wrangling their way up the sink drain. STOMP, SMACK, SCREAM, REPEAT.

These days, Thanksgiving is a much more muted affair by comparison, with roast turkey, fried rice, ceviche, and a full arsenal of Raid under the sink at the ready (however unlikely the threat of infestation). The biggest preoccupation now is how to repurpose all the leftovers, since my family often cooks enough food for three times the number of actual guests. Stuffing shredded turkey into a pot pie is an excellent way to give it a second life while still presenting it as a fresh meal. If you're making this out of season, chicken is a fitting substitute.

1 disk Spinach Pie Dough (page 162)

2 disks Whole Wheat Cheddar Chive Pie Dough (page 165)

TURKEY POT PIE FILLING

5 tablespoons (76 grams) unsalted butter

2 garlic cloves, minced

1 yellow onion, diced (about 1 cup)

1 small sweet potato, peeled and cut into ¼-inch dice (about 1 cup)

3 large carrots, peeled and cut into ¼-inch dice (about 1 cup)

3 celery stalks, cut into ¼-inch dice (about 1 cup)

1 teaspoon dried thyme

1. To make the turkey pot pie filling, melt the butter in a Dutch oven over medium-high heat. Add the garlic, onion, sweet potato, carrots, celery, thyme, and rosemary and sauté until the onion is translucent and the vegetables tender, about 10 minutes. Season with salt and pepper.

2. Sprinkle in the flour and cook until the flour turns a golden amber, stirring frequently. As you continue to stir, slowly drizzle in the broth. Gradually add the milk and cook, stirring, until the sauce is thickened, about 7 minutes. Add the frozen peas and the turkey, season with salt and pepper, and cook 5 minutes more. Cool completely before filling the pie. (The filling can be made ahead and refrigerated.)

3. Roll the spinach dough disk into a 13-inch square. Roll the dough onto the rolling pin and unfurl it onto a sheet of parchment paper. Using a ruler as a straight edge and a rolling pastry wheel, cut the square into ¼-inch strips. Slide a flat baking sheet under the parchment and place the dough in the refrigerator.

recipe continues

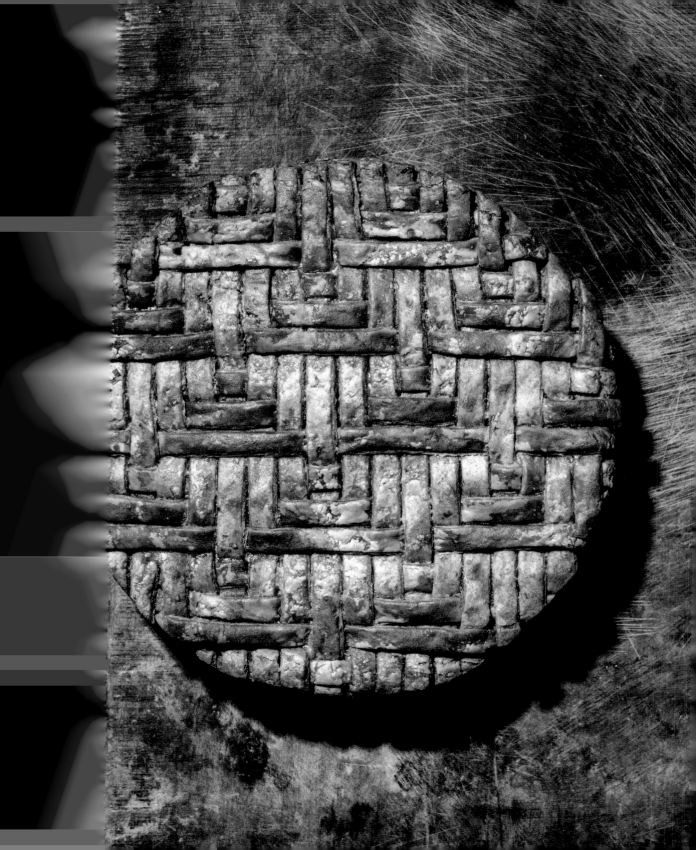

1 teaspoon dried rosemary

Kosher salt and freshly ground black pepper

⅓ cup (47 grams) all-purpose flour

2 cups (474 milliliters) chicken broth

1 cup (237 milliliters) milk

½ cup (75 grams) frozen peas

2 cups (8 ounces/227 grams) shredded cooked turkey

PYRAMID WEAVE DESIGN PROCESS

Parchment paper

Ruler

Rolling pastry wheel

Paring knife

4. Repeat this process with 1 whole wheat Cheddar chive dough disk. Slide the parchment sheet of Cheddar chive dough strips on top of the spinach strips and chill the strips for at least 10 minutes before proceeding.

5. Place the sheet of Cheddar chive dough so that the strips lay vertically and count out 23 strips. Set aside any extras. Set the sheet of spinach strips nearby.

6. The basic 6-row woven unit of the pattern is as follows:

ROW 1: On the Cheddar sheet, starting from the left, leave the first five strips and fold back the sixth. Continue and repeat leaving five, folding one twice more. Lay a perpendicular spinach strip along the middle and unfold the vertical Cheddar strips over it.

FOLDED CHEDDAR STRIPS: 6, 12, 18

UNFOLDED CHEDDAR STRIPS: 1, 2, 3, 4, 5, 7, 8, 9, 10, 11, 13, 14, 15, 16, 17, 19, 20, 21, 22, 23

ROW 2: Starting from the left, leave the first four strips and fold back the next three. Count out three strips and fold back the next three. Count out another three strips and fold back three. Lay a perpendicular spinach strip, nestling it close to the first spinach strip, and unfold all the vertical strips over it.

FOLDED CHEDDAR STRIPS: 5, 6, 7, 11, 12, 13, 17, 18, 19

UNFOLDED CHEDDAR STRIPS: 1, 2, 3, 4, 8, 9, 10, 14, 15, 16, 20, 21, 22, 23

ROW 3: Starting from the left, leave the first three strips and fold back the next five. Skip the next strip and then fold back five. Leave another strip and fold back the next five. Lay a perpendicular spinach strip and unfold all the vertical strips over it.

FOLDED CHEDDAR STRIPS: 4, 5, 6, 7, 8, 10, 11, 12, 13, 14, 16, 17, 18, 19, 20

UNFOLDED CHEDDAR STRIPS: 1, 2, 3, 9, 15, 21, 22, 23

ROW 4: Leave the first two strips and fold back the third. Skip the next five strips and fold back the sixth. Count another five strips and fold the sixth strip back. Count five more strips and fold the sixth strip back. Lay a perpendicular spinach strip and unfold all the vertical strips over it.

recipe continues

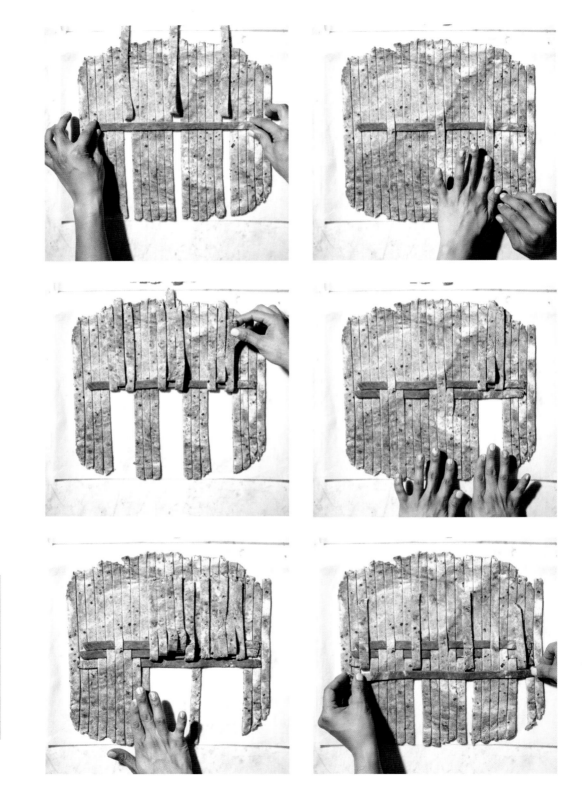

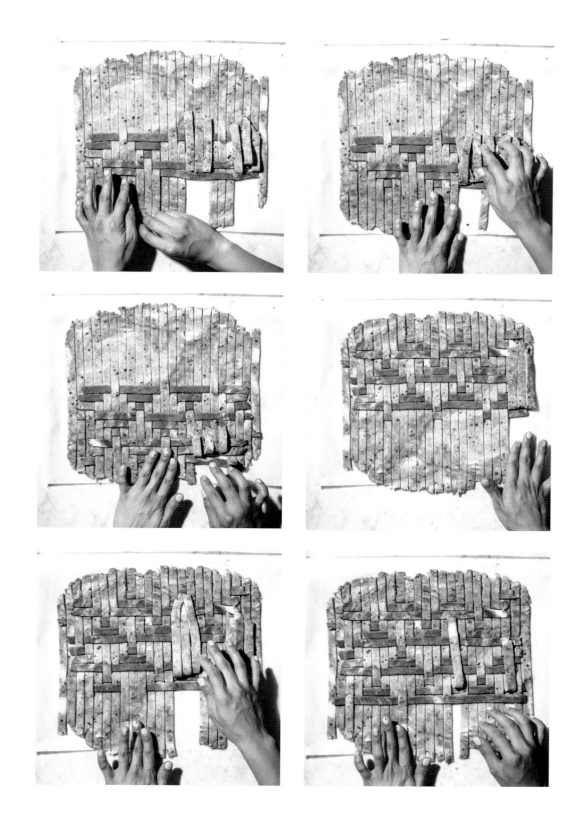

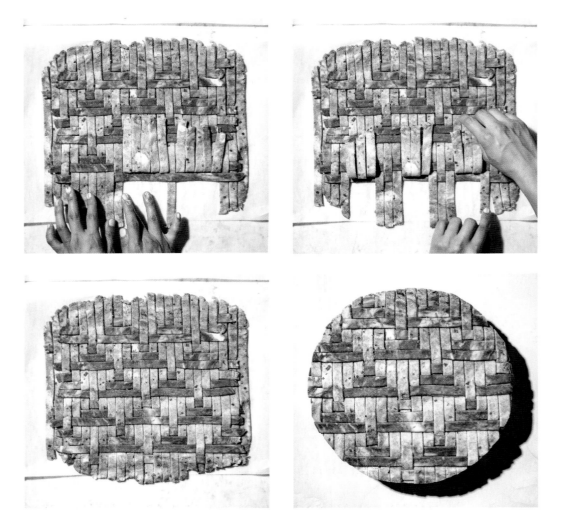

FOLDED CHEDDAR STRIPS: 3, 9, 15, 21
UNFOLDED CHEDDAR STRIPS: 1, 2, 4, 5, 6, 7, 8, 10, 11, 12, 13, 14, 16, 17, 18, 19, 20, 22, 23

ROW 5: Leave the first strip and fold back the next three. Skip three strips and fold back the next three. Skip the next three strips and fold back the following three. Lay a perpendicular spinach strip and unfold all the vertical strips over it.

FOLDED CHEDDAR STRIPS: 2, 3, 4, 8, 9, 10, 14, 15, 16, 20, 21, 22
UNFOLDED CHEDDAR STRIPS: 1, 5, 6, 7, 11, 12, 13, 17, 18, 19, 23

ROW 6: Fold the first five strips back, skip the sixth, and fold back the next five strips. Skip another strip, fold back the next five, skip a strip, and fold back the last five.

FOLDED CHEDDAR STRIPS: 1, 2, 3, 4, 5, 7, 8, 9, 10, 11, 13, 14, 15, 16, 17, 19, 20, 21, 22, 23

UNFOLDED CHEDDAR STRIP: 6, 12, 18

7. Repeat the weaving process for rows 1 to 6 until the vertical strips end.

8. Rotate the parchment 180 degrees. Repeat step 6 in reverse order; following instructions for rows 6 through 1.

9. Once you've completed the full weave, slide a flat baking sheet under the parchment and freeze the pie top for at least 30 minutes or until it can be easily lifted as one piece. Once the pie top has frozen solid, it can be wrapped well and used to top a pie at a later time. A well-sealed pie top will keep in the freezer for up to 3 months. Handle frozen pie tops gently as they can shatter.

10. While the weave freezes, roll the remaining disk of Cheddar dough into a 14-inch circle. Roll the dough onto the rolling pin and unfurl it over a 9-inch pie pan. Taking the edges of the dough, gently ease the dough into the pan, nestling it into the inner elbows of the pie pan. Trim the excess dough with kitchen shears to create a 1-inch overhang. Fold the overhang back under, creating an elevated edge.

11. Fill the pie shell with the turkey filling and lightly brush the edge of the pie with water.

12. Remove the frozen weave from the freezer, pick it up as one solid piece, and lay it centered on the surface of your filled pie. Let it sit for a few minutes to thaw slightly and settle. Press to seal the edges and run a paring knife around the edge to trim the excess dough.

13. Chill the entire pie in the freezer until the oven has come to temperature. The pie can be frozen solid before baking or simply chilled through, about 20 minutes.

14. Preheat the oven to 425°F. Line a rimmed baking sheet with parchment paper.

recipe continues

15. When the oven has come to temperature, place the chilled pie on the prepared baking sheet. Bake for 25 minutes, then rotate the pie 180 degrees and lower the oven temperature to 400°F. If the edges are already brown, cover with a shield. Continue baking until the filling is bubbling rapidly and the top crust looks baked through in the center, checking every 30 minutes to rotate the pie and cover lightly with foil as necessary, 60 to 80 total minutes. (If baking from frozen, add 30 to 45 minutes to the bake time.)

16. Cool the pie completely on a rack before slicing and serving.

SUGGESTED SUBSTITUTIONS

Dough alternatives: Basic (page 134), Carrot (page 150), Spinach Pie Dough with poppy seeds (page 162)

Filling alternative: Chicken

NOTE

The filling can be made 1 or 2 days in advance and stored in the refrigerator.

SEEING IS BEWEAVING

I got talked into my first ever backpacking trip a few summers ago. Day one alone included trekking thirteen miles (I was told we were going to do eight), scrabbling up rocks with infuriatingly heavy packs (schlepping is the dumbest), discovering some truly wonderful sights (okay, nature is cool), and finally posting up in a magical meadow for the night with no one around for miles (BUT ARE THERE BEARS? is probably why I couldn't sleep).

I've never been the most outdoorsy person, so I had serious concerns about dying on the mountain, leaving my husband behind to drag my body back to civilization. And things did get dicey. My face swelled to the size of a midsummer cantaloupe the second morning and my feet pitched a fit until I swore off nature forever. But reaching the mountain summit—even at a crawl—and seeing the brown trailhead sign reappear at the end of the trip somehow made a believer out of me. Not that I've done another trip, but I would allow someone the opportunity to convince me . . .

I'm not saying this woven pattern is as arduous as a twenty-mile expedition while lugging a fifty-pound pack, but it's not exactly a stroll in the park. Stick with it, though, even when the doughing gets rough, and the satisfaction of that final pie weave may just convert you. You'll see.

2 disks Basic Pie Dough (page 134)

1 disk Blueberry Pie Dough (page 144)

1 disk Butterfly Pea Flower Pie Dough (page 147)

PLUM BASIL FILLING

½ ounce (14 grams) fresh basil leaves

1 cup (198 grams) granulated sugar

1 teaspoon kosher salt

2 pounds (907 grams) plums, pitted and cut into 1-inch chunks

⅓ cup (38 grams) tapioca starch

1. On a floured surface, roll one disk of basic dough into a 15-inch square. Roll the dough onto the rolling pin and unfurl it onto a sheet of parchment paper. Using a ruler as a straight edge and a rolling pastry wheel, cut the square into ¼-inch strips. You should have at least 24 strips. Slide a flat baking sheet under the parchment and place the dough in the refrigerator to keep cold while proceeding with the design process.

2. Roll the disk of blueberry dough into a 14-inch square. Roll the dough onto the rolling pin and unfurl it onto a sheet of parchment paper. Using a ruler as a straight edge and a rolling pastry wheel, cut the square into ¼-inch strips.

3. Repeat this process with the butterfly pea flower dough.

4. Carefully stack these sheets of parchment on the tray containing the white strips and return to the refrigerator to chill for 5 to 10 minutes before proceeding.

5. Remove the chilled dough strips from the refrigerator. Place the sheet of white dough in front of you so that the strips are configured vertically and count 24 strips. Remove and set aside any extra strips.

recipe continues

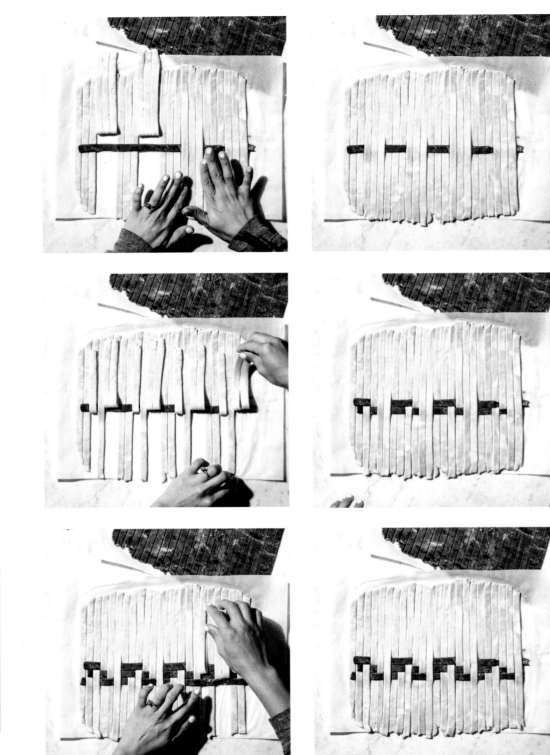

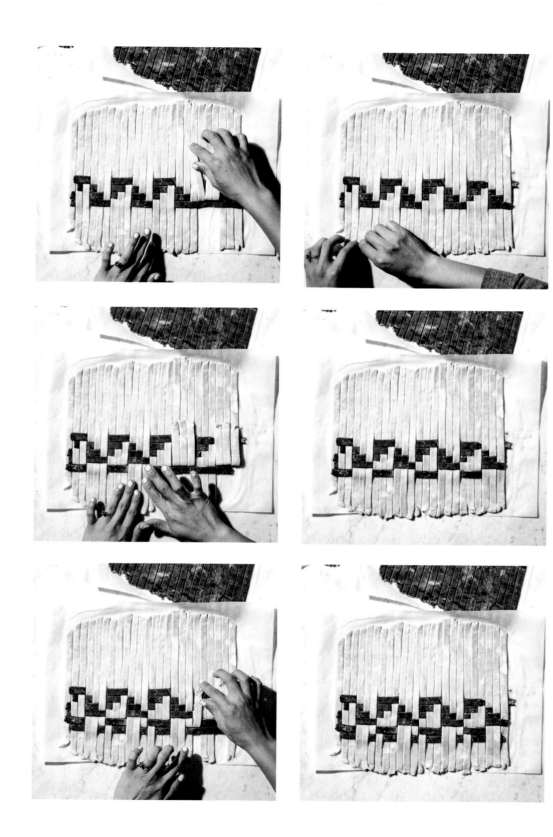

Parchment paper

Baking sheets

Ruler

Rolling pastry wheel

Paring knife

6. (If your dough becomes warm and melty at any point, you can slide a baking sheet under the parchment and pop the whole operation into the refrigerator for 5 minutes to chill before resuming with weaving.) The basic 8-row woven unit for this pattern is as follows:

ROW 1: Starting from the left, count out three strips and fold back the next three. Count out three more and fold back the next three. Continue in this pattern until you've exhausted the white strips. Lay a perpendicular blue strip across the middle and unfold all the white strips over it.

FOLDED WHITE STRIPS: 4, 5, 6, 10, 11, 12, 16, 17, 18, 22, 23, 24
UNFOLDED WHITE STRIPS: 1, 2, 3, 7, 8, 9, 13, 14, 15, 19, 20, 21
HORIZONTAL STRIP: blue

ROW 2: Starting from the left, count out two strips and fold back the third. Leave the fourth strip and fold back the next two strips. Continue and repeat leaving two, folding one, leaving one, folding two. Lay a perpendicular blue strip, nestled closely to the first blue strip, and unfold all the white strips over it.

FOLDED WHITE STRIPS: 3, 5, 6, 9, 11, 12, 15, 17, 18, 21, 23, 24
UNFOLDED WHITE STRIPS: 1, 2, 4, 7, 8, 10, 13, 14, 16, 19, 20, 22
HORIZONTAL STRIP: blue

ROW 3: Count out one strip, fold back two. Count out the next two strips and fold back one. Continue and repeat leaving one, folding two, leaving two, folding one.

FOLDED WHITE STRIPS: 2, 3, 6, 8, 9, 12, 14, 15, 18, 20, 21
UNFOLDED WHITE STRIPS: 1, 4, 5, 7, 10, 11, 13, 16, 17, 19, 22, 23, 24
HORIZONTAL STRIP: blue

ROW 4: Fold back the first three strips and leave the next three. Continue folding three, leaving three. Lay a perpendicular blue strip across the middle, and unfold all the white strips over it.

FOLDED STRIPS: 1, 2, 3, 7, 8, 9, 13, 14, 15, 19, 20, 21
UNFOLDED STRIPS: 4, 5, 6, 10, 11, 12, 16, 17, 18, 22, 23, 24
HORIZONTAL STRIP: blue

ROW 5: Count out three strips and fold back the next three. Count out three more and fold back the next three. Continue leaving three, folding three. Lay a perpendicular purple strip across the middle and unfold all the white strips over it.

recipe continues

FOLDED WHITE STRIPS: 4, 5, 6, 10, 11, 12, 16, 17, 18, 22, 23, 24
UNFOLDED WHITE STRIPS: 1, 2, 3, 7, 8, 9, 13, 14, 15, 19, 20, 21
HORIZONTAL STRIP: purple

ROW 6: Fold back the first strip, leave the next two. Fold back the following two strips and leave the next one. Continue and repeat folding one, leaving two, folding two, leaving one. Lay down a perpendicular purple strip and unfold all the white strips over it.

FOLDED WHITE STRIPS: 1, 4, 5, 7, 10, 11, 13, 16, 17, 19, 22, 23
UNFOLDED WHITE STRIPS: 2, 3, 6, 8, 9, 12, 14, 15, 18, 20, 21, 24
HORIZONTAL STRIP: purple

ROW 7: Fold back the first two strips, leave the next one. Fold back the following strip and leave the next two. Continue and repeat folding two, leaving one, folding one, leaving two. Lay down a perpendicular purple strip and unfold all the white strips over it.

FOLDED WHITE STRIPS: 1, 2, 4, 7, 8, 10, 13, 14, 16, 19, 21, 22
UNFOLDED WHITE STRIPS: 3, 5, 6, 9, 11, 12, 15, 17, 18, 20, 23, 24
HORIZONTAL STRIP: purple

ROW 8: Fold back the first three strips, leave the next three. Continue and repeat folding three, leaving three. Lay down a perpendicular purple strip and unfold all the white strips over it.

FOLDED WHITE STRIPS: 1, 2, 3, 7, 8, 9, 13, 14, 15, 19, 20, 21
UNFOLDED WHITE STRIPS: 4, 5, 6, 10, 11, 12, 16, 17, 18, 22, 23, 24
HORIZONTAL STRIP: purple

7. Rotate the parchment 180 degrees and repeat the weave in reverse order, following instructions for rows 8 through 1.

8. Once you've completed the full weave, slide a flat baking sheet under the parchment and freeze the pie top for at least 30 minutes, or until it can be easily lifted as one piece. Once the pie top has frozen solid, it can be wrapped well and used to top a pie at a later time. A well-sealed pie top will keep in the freezer for up to 3 months. Handle frozen pie tops gently, as they can shatter.

9. Roll the second disk of basic dough into a 14-inch circle. Roll the dough onto the rolling pin and unfurl it over a 9-inch

recipe continues

pie pan. Taking the edges of the dough, gently ease the dough into the pan, nestling it into the inner elbows of the pie pan. Trim the excess dough with kitchen shears to create a 1-inch overhang. Fold the overhang back under, creating an elevated edge.

10. To prepare the plum basil filling, combine the basil, sugar, and salt in a food processor and blitz until the basil has been fully incorporated into the sugar. Put the basil sugar, plums, and tapioca starch in a large bowl and gently fold with a spatula to coat the fruit.

11. Scoop the filling into the prepared pie shell. Use a pastry brush to lightly brush the edge of the pie with water.

12. Remove the frozen weave from the freezer, pick it up as one solid piece, and lay it centered on the surface of your filled pie. Let it sit for a few minutes to thaw slightly and settle. Press to seal the edges and run a paring knife around the edge to trim the excess dough.

13. Chill the entire pie in the freezer until the oven has come to temperature. The pie can be frozen solid before baking or simply chilled through, about 20 minutes.

14. Preheat the oven to 400°F. Line a rimmed baking sheet with parchment paper.

15. When the oven has come to temperature, place the chilled pie on the prepared baking sheet. Bake for 25 minutes, then rotate the pie 180 degrees and lower the oven temperature to 350°F. Lightly cover the top of the pie with foil to preserve the vibrancy of the colors. Remove the foil for the last 10 to 15 minutes of baking to allow the top crust to cook through. Continue baking until the filling is bubbling rapidly and the top crust is baked through in the center, checking every 30 minutes to rotate the pie, 80 to 100 total minutes. (If baking from frozen, add 30 to 45 minutes to the bake time.)

16. Cool the pie completely on a rack before slicing and serving.

SUGGESTED SUBSTITUTIONS

Dough alternatives: Beet (page 138), Black Sesame (page 141), Carrot (page 150), Cornflower (page 152), Dragon Fruit (page 155)

NOTES

If you're just beginning your pie design journey, I don't recommend this weave as your first foray. It requires a little brain stretching and a fair amount of time, so unless you're wholly committed to setting the bar high and promise to absolve me of any of your frustration, I suggest you leave this pie for later down the baking road.

The trimmed dough scraps can be baked as beautiful woven pie cookies (see page 130). The extra dough strips can be gently pressed into a disk, wrapped, chilled, and re-rolled once more into marbled dough for a pie like Caught Off Shard (page 264).

BLOCK AND AWE

While I don't have any firsthand experience with the art form, I'm an avid admirer of block printing. I could easily fritter away my livelihood purchasing textiles featuring repetitive geometric motifs in idiosyncratic color combinations—aside from potato chips, they're my most compulsive impulse buys. To maintain a semblance of financial solvency, I resort to creating my own block print–inspired goods through the more economical medium of pie dough. I may not be able to hang my creations on the wall, but enveloping a pie in a peppy print is a pretty awesome consolation prize.

1 disk Beet Pie Dough (page 138)

2 disks Nutella Pie Dough (page 158)

CHERRY FILLING

6 cups (2½ pounds/1.1 kilograms) pitted fresh or frozen sweet cherries, such as Bing or Rainier

¾ cup (149 grams) granulated sugar

⅓ cup (38 grams) tapioca starch

1 teaspoon kosher salt

1 teaspoon fresh lemon juice

SEMICIRCLE TILE DESIGN NEEDS

Parchment paper

1-inch circle cutter

1 small bowl of water

Pastry brush

Paring knife

1. On a floured surface, roll the disk of beet dough into a 12-inch circle. Roll the dough onto the rolling pin and unfurl it onto a sheet of parchment paper. Using a 1-inch circle cutter, punch out at least 70 shapes. Remove the dough scraps. Use a paring knife to cut each circle in half. If your knife is sticking to the dough or not cutting cleanly, tap the blade in flour before slicing.

2. Slide a flat baking sheet under the parchment and chill the dough in the refrigerator.

3. Roll one disk of Nutella dough into a 13-inch circle. Roll the dough onto the rolling pin and unfurl it onto a sheet of parchment paper.

4. Gently lay a ruler horizontally across the center of the Nutella dough as a straight line reference. Remove the beet shapes from the refrigerator. Starting from the left, brush a small section of the Nutella dough with water and place a beet semicircle with the straight edge flush against the ruler. Lay its mirror image just above with the curved edges of the semicircles touching. Next, place a beet semicircle upright with its straight edge to the left. Place the mirror image of this last piece to the right with its straight edge facing right. Continue placing beet semicircle tiles in this alternating pattern until an entire row has been completed.

5. Proceed with placing rows of tiles above and below, alternating the directional placement of the tiles, until the surface of the Nutella dough has been largely covered.

recipe continues

6. Use a paring knife or shape cutter to cut one or two vent holes. I like to follow the tile pattern with semicircle vents to camouflage the cutouts, but take liberties to ventilate as preferred. I often forget this step, and the suffocated pie filling will give me a piece of its mind during baking by puffing up the pie top so severely as to cause an unsightly crack or a bulbous baked surface. Best to let the filling air its grievances freely.

7. Slide a flat baking sheet under the parchment and freeze the pie top for at least 30 minutes or until it can be easily lifted as one piece. Once the pie top has frozen solid, it can be wrapped well and used to top a pie at a later time. A well-sealed pie top will keep in the freezer for up to 3 months. Handle frozen pie tops gently, as they can shatter.

8. Roll the second disk of Nutella dough into a 14-inch circle. Roll the dough onto the rolling pin and unfurl it over a 9-inch pie pan. Taking the edges of the dough, gently ease the dough into the pan, nestling it into the inner elbows of the pie pan. Trim the excess dough with kitchen shears to create a 1-inch overhang. Fold the overhang back under, creating an elevated edge.

9. To prepare the cherry filling, combine all the ingredients in a large bowl and fold with a spatula to coat the fruit in the sugar mixture.

10. Scoop the filling into the prepared pie shell, doming the fruit in the center. Lightly brush water around the edge of the pie.

11. Remove the frozen pie top from the freezer, pick it up as one solid piece, and lay the frozen dough centered on the surface of your filled pie. Let it sit for a few minutes to thaw slightly and settle. Press to seal the edges and run a paring knife around the edge to trim the excess dough.

12. Chill the entire pie in the freezer until the oven has come to temperature. The pie can be frozen solid before baking or simply chilled through, about 20 minutes.

13. Preheat the oven to 400°F. Line a rimmed baking sheet with parchment.

recipe continues

14. When the oven has come to temperature, remove the pie from the freezer and place it on the prepared baking sheet. Bake the pie for 25 minutes, then rotate the pie 180 degrees and lower the oven temperature to 350°F. If the edges are already brown, cover with a shield. If the beet tiles begin to brown excessively, rest a sheet of foil lightly on top. Continue baking until the filling is bubbling in the center, checking every 30 minutes to rotate the pie and adjust the shields as necessary, 80 to 100 total minutes. (If baking from frozen, add 30 to 45 minutes to the bake time.)

15. Cool the pie completely on a rack before slicing and serving.

SUGGESTED SUBSTITUTIONS

Dough alternatives: Basic (page 134), Black Sesame (page 141), Blueberry (page 144), Butterfly Pea Flower (page 147), Cornflower (page 152), Dragon Fruit (page 155)

RANK AND TILE

This design is inspired by Portuguese buildings adorned with azulejos, intricately painted tile work that sparks a thousand daydreams with its colorful allure. I vividly recall wandering the streets of Porto, spellbound and wondering: (1) if there was a limit to how many pastéis de natas one can consume in a day and (2) how to return as a tile painter in my next life. And in the magical ways of dreams-turned-reality, here I am a decade later, crafting tile work of my own after all; a pursuit at times charmed and at other times intensely toilsome, but always worthtile.

1 disk Carrot Pie Dough (page 150)

2 disks Spinach Pie Dough (page 162) with poppy seeds

MUSHROOM LEEK FILLING

3 tablespoons olive oil

4 garlic cloves, minced

½ tablespoon fresh rosemary leaves, roughly chopped

5 cups (24 ounces/681 grams) cremini mushrooms, cut into ¼-inch slices

Kosher salt

2 tablespoons (28 grams) unsalted butter

2 parsnips, peeled and chopped

1 large gold potato, peeled and chopped

1 small apple, peeled, cored, and chopped

3 large leeks (1 pound/454 grams), light green and white parts only, rinsed well and thinly sliced

1. On a floured surface, roll one disk of carrot dough into a 13-inch circle. Roll the dough onto the rolling pin and unfurl it onto a sheet of parchment paper.

2. Slide a flat baking sheet under the parchment and place the dough in the refrigerator to chill.

3. Roll one disk of spinach poppy seed dough into a 12-inch square. Roll the dough onto the rolling pin and unfurl it onto a sheet of parchment paper. Using a rectangle cutter, punch out at least 40 shapes. Remove the dough scraps to bake as cookies (see page 130) or to re-roll once more for another design.

4. Using one corner of the rectangle cutter, punch out an isosceles right triangle along one of the rectangle's short edges, then use a paring knife to cut down the middle, creating two pairs of mirror-image shapes, a right-angle trapezoid, and a triangle in each pair. Tap the cutter and paring knife in flour to prevent sticking.

5. Slide a flat baking sheet under the parchment and place the dough in the refrigerator to chill for 5 to 10 minutes.

6. Remove the rolled carrot dough and the spinach shapes from the refrigerator. Lay a ruler horizontally across the center of the carrot dough and lightly brush water on a small section starting from the left. Line a short edge of a spinach right triangle against the ruler with its hypotenuse facing left. Lay a quadrilateral next with its longest edge facing right and pointy end touching the ruler. Continue laying an entire row

recipe continues

PIE DESIGNS

259

Freshly ground black pepper

Parchment paper

1½ × 1-inch rectangle cutter

Small bowl of water

Pastry brush

Paring knife

of spinach pieces, alternating between right triangles and quadrilaterals, brushing water as needed to secure the dough.

7. Remove the ruler and set it aside. Rotate the parchment with carrot dough 180 degrees and lay another horizontal row of spinach shapes in the same pattern as the first row, alternating between right triangles and quadrilaterals.

8. Repeat this 2-row pattern until the entire surface of the carrot dough is covered.

9. Slide a flat baking sheet under the parchment and freeze the pie top for at least 30 minutes or until it can be easily lifted as one piece. Once the pie top has frozen solid, it can be wrapped well and used to top a pie at a later time. A well-sealed pie top will keep in the freezer for up to 3 months. Handle frozen pie tops gently, as they can shatter.

10. Roll the second disk of carrot dough into a 14-inch circle. Roll the dough onto the rolling pin and unfurl it over a 9-inch pie pan. Taking the edges of the dough, gently ease the dough into the pan, nestling it into the inner elbows of the pie pan. Trim the excess dough with kitchen shears to create a 1-inch overhang. Fold the overhang back under, creating an elevated edge.

11. To prepare the mushroom leek filling, heat the oil in a large skillet over medium-high heat and lightly fry the garlic and rosemary, about 1 minute. Lay a single layer of mushroom slices in the pan and cook without agitating until browned, about 5 minutes. Turn the mushrooms over, season with salt, and brown the other side, until most of the liquid is cooked out and the mushrooms have developed a deep brown crust. Remove to a plate. Repeat to cook the rest of the mushrooms. Set aside.

12. Melt the butter in the same skillet over medium-high heat and brown the parsnips, potato, and apple, stirring occasionally, about 10 minutes. Add the leeks, season generously with salt and pepper, and sauté until all the vegetables are tender, about 10 minutes. Add the browned mushrooms and cook 1 more minute. Season to taste with salt and pepper.

13. Scoop the filling into the prepared pie shell.

recipe continues

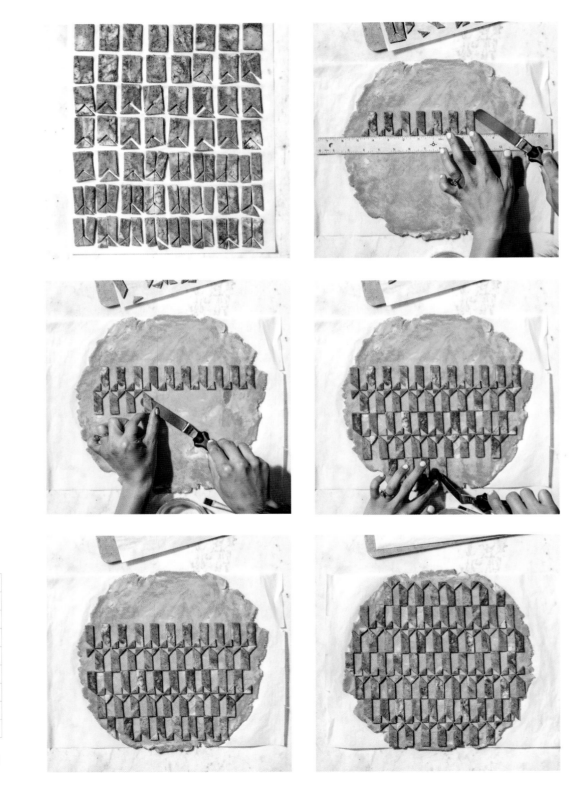

14. Remove the frozen pie top from the freezer. Use a paring knife or shape cutter to cut one or two vent holes. Lightly brush water around the edge of the pie and lay the frozen dough centered on the surface of your filled pie. Let it sit for a few minutes to thaw slightly and settle. Press to seal the edges and run a paring knife around the edge to trim the excess dough.

15. Chill the entire pie in the freezer until the oven has come to temperature. The pie can be frozen solid before baking or simply chilled through, about 20 minutes.

16. Preheat the oven to 400°F. Line a rimmed baking sheet with parchment.

17. When the oven has come to temperature, remove the pie from the freezer and place it on the prepared baking sheet. Bake the pie for 25 minutes, then rotate the pie 180 degrees and lower the oven temperature to 350°F. If the edges are already brown, cover with a shield. If the spinach tiles begin to brown excessively, rest a sheet of foil lightly on top. Continue baking until the filling is bubbling in the center, checking every 30 minutes to rotate the pie and adjust the shields as necessary, 50 to 75 total minutes. (If baking from frozen, add 30 to 45 minutes to the bake time.)

18. Cool the pie completely on a rack before slicing and serving.

SUGGESTED SUBSTITUTIONS

Dough alternatives: Basic (page 134), Beet (page 138), Whole Wheat Cheddar Chive (page 165)

NOTE

The filling can be made 1 or 2 days in advance and stored in the refrigerator.

CAUGHT OFF SHARD

At this point, you might have an inkling that I have butterfingers (and I'm now realizing this applies figuratively and literally). I drop things constantly, always to horrific effect. I once lost my grip on a boiling hot pie so badly that the contents went from the oven to the floor to the ceiling and then back to the floor. I've also been known to fumble tangram tarts in professional test kitchens shortly before I'm due on set to start filming. It's all very pie stakes.

These experiences, though, did not prepare me for someone else doing the toppling. I had been recruited to assemble a dessert table for the wedding of dear friends. Having delivered an assortment of pies and tarts to the reception locale the previous day, I arrived shortly after the ceremony to set up. God only knows what happened overnight, but several of the tarts were completely and utterly shattered. Like my heart.

I sobbed, watched my other friends try to put the pieces back together, consumed a lot of tequila, and then eventually turned those crumpled ruins into a design. Similar in technique and process to Happy as a Gram (page 51), this design has the added bonus of repurposing leftover dough. Scraps that may be otherwise discarded survive to live in a colorful, renewed capacity. Lemons to lemonade. Shard times to shard designs (and really bad rhymes and other such crimes).

1 disk Marbled Pie Dough (page 160)

2 disks Basic Pie Dough (page 134)

BLUEBERRY PINEAPPLE FILLING

4 cups 1-inch fresh pineapple chunks (about 1½ pounds/680 grams)

2 cups (12 ounces) fresh or frozen blueberries

⅔ cup (132 grams) granulated sugar

¼ cup (28 grams) tapioca starch

1 tablespoon fresh lime juice

1 teaspoon kosher salt

1. On a floured surface, roll the disk of marbled dough into a circle, rectangle, nebulous galactic blob, whatever! You have some flexibility with this design. Roll the dough onto the rolling pin and unfurl it onto a sheet of parchment paper. Slide a flat baking sheet under the parchment and place the dough in the refrigerator to chill.

2. Roll the disk of basic dough into a 13-inch circle. Roll the dough onto the rolling pin and unfurl it onto a sheet of parchment paper.

3. Remove the marbled dough from the refrigerator and use a chef's knife to cut a variety of three- and four-sided shapes.

4. Lightly brush a small section of the rolled basic dough with water and place several of the marbled shapes on it, fitting them together like a puzzle but leaving some space between the pieces.

5. Continue brushing water and adhering shapes, working a section at a time, until the entire surface of the white pie dough is covered or you run out of marbled dough.

recipe continues

265

Parchment paper

Chef's knife

Paring knife

Pastry brush

Small bowl of water

Dough alternatives: If you have any miscellaneous small disks of leftover colored dough from other designs, this is a prime opportunity to utilize them. Simply roll them out as instructed in step 1 and proceed with the directions. Otherwise, you can also substitute one complete disk of any dough.

6. Using a paring knife or a small shape cutter, cut a small vent hole. Slide a flat baking sheet under the parchment and freeze the pie top for at least 30 minutes, or until it can be easily lifted as one piece. Once the pie top has frozen solid, it can be wrapped well and used to top a pie at a later time. A well-sealed pie top will keep in the freezer for up to 3 months. Handle frozen pie tops gently, as they can shatter.

7. Roll the second disk of basic dough into a 14-inch circle. Roll the dough onto the rolling pin and unfurl it over a 9-inch pie pan. Taking the edges of the dough, gently ease the dough into the pan, nestling it into the inner elbows of the pie pan. Trim the excess dough with kitchen shears to create a 1-inch overhang. Fold the overhang back under, creating an elevated edge.

8. To prepare the blueberry pineapple filling, combine all the ingredients in a large bowl and gently fold with a spatula to coat the fruit.

9. Scoop the filling into the prepared pie shell. Use a pastry brush to lightly brush water around the edge of the pie.

10. Remove the frozen tangram top from the freezer, pick it up as one solid piece, and lay it centered on the surface of your filled pie. Let it sit for a few minutes to thaw slightly and settle. Press to seal the edges, and run a paring knife around the edge to trim the excess dough.

11. Chill the entire pie in the freezer until the oven has come to temperature. The pie can be frozen solid before baking or simply chilled through, about 20 minutes.

12. Preheat the oven to 400°F. Line a baking sheet with parchment.

13. When the oven has come to temperature, place the chilled pie on the prepared baking sheet. Bake for 25 minutes, then rotate the pie 180 degrees and lower the oven temperature to 350°F. If the edges are already brown, cover with a shield. Continue baking until the filling is bubbling rapidly and the top crust looks baked through in the center, checking every 30 minutes to rotate the pie and cover lightly with foil as necessary, 80 to 100 total minutes. (If baking from frozen, add 30 to 45 minutes to the bake time.)

14. Cool the pie completely on a rack before slicing and serving.

HERB APPEAL

After a lifetime of cultivating my black thumb, I got the wild idea to start gardening. Our house came with a planter box in the yard, which we had been putting to really great use by growing a feral safari of weeds and other alarming green things. We cleared the hazard zone and planted a variety of herbs, lettuces, and strawberries. Chalk it up to beginner's luck or simply starting with the easiest crops, but our garden took off. We were soon drowning in a sea of salad and pesto.

This pie was initially about survival. It was a non-frittata, non-salad fridge-clear-out strategy to utilize the drawer dregs and the surplus of herbs. But the result was so fragrant and full of flavor that it quickly made its way into the regular dinnertime rotation. One day I'm going to be a tan and wrinkly old lady living in her beach cottage by the ocean with a brick-lined path leading to her herb garden, and I'll still be making this pie because this recipe is good enough to withstand the test of thyme.

2 disks Carrot Pie Dough (page 150)

SAUSAGE AND SUN-DRIED TOMATO FILLING

1 tablespoon olive oil

1½ pounds (680 grams) hot Italian sausage, casings removed

4 garlic cloves, minced

1 white onion, cut into ¼-inch dice (about 1 cup)

1 large carrot, peeled and cut into ¼-inch dice (about ½ cup)

1 teaspoon dried oregano

½ teaspoon red pepper flakes (optional)

Kosher salt and freshly ground black pepper

1 large ripe tomato, cut into ¼-inch dice (about 1 cup)

1. Heat the oil in a large skillet over medium-high heat. Add the sausage and cook, breaking it up, until browned, 10 to 12 minutes. Remove the sausage to a bowl with a slotted spoon and set aside.

2. In the same skillet over medium-high heat, sauté the garlic, onion, carrot, oregano, red pepper flakes (if using), and salt and pepper to taste until the vegetables are just tender, 8 to 10 minutes. Return the sausage to the pan and add the chopped tomato, olives, and sun-dried tomatoes. Cook for 2 to 3 minutes to heat everything through, stirring often. Season to taste with salt and pepper. Set aside to cool.

3. Cut the chives into 1-inch segments. Pick the rosemary into leaves and the thyme into small sprigs. Separate by kind and set aside.

4. On a floured surface, roll one disk of carrot dough into an 11 × 13-inch rectangle. Roll the dough onto the rolling pin and unfurl it onto a sheet of parchment paper. Mentally divide the rectangle into four even sections. Working one section at a time, lightly brush the egg white mixture on the dough and apply one type of herb per section in a scattered, random pattern, pressing gently to secure. (If your dough becomes warm and melty at any point, slide a flat baking sheet under

recipe continues

½ cup pitted green olives, sliced into thirds

½ cup sun-dried tomatoes (see Note)

EGG WASH

1 egg white whisked with 1 tablespoon water

HERB TILE DESIGN NEEDS

10 fresh chives

40 small fresh sage leaves

3 fresh rosemary sprigs

3 fresh thyme sprigs

Parchment paper

1½ × 1-inch rectangle cutter

Pastry brush

Paring knife

the parchment and chill in the refrigerator for 5 to 10 minutes before resuming.)

5. Use the rectangle cutter to punch out at least 65 herb tiles. Press firmly and use a paring knife if necessary to cut through the leaves. Line up the tiles on another sheet of parchment.

6. Place the tiles in the refrigerator to keep cool. If you plan to chill the tiles for longer than 1 hour, cover the baking sheet to prevent the dough from drying out.

7. Roll the second disk of dough into a 14-inch circle. Roll the dough onto the rolling pin and unfurl it over a 9-inch pie pan. Taking the edges of the dough, gently ease the dough into the pan, nestling it into the inner elbows of the pie pan. Trim the excess dough with kitchen shears to create a 1-inch overhang. Fold the overhang back under, creating an elevated edge.

8. Scoop the cooled sausage filling into the pie shell. Lightly brush the edge with the remaining egg white mixture or water.

9. Arrange the herb tiles on the surface of the pie in a herringbone pattern, lining short edges against long edges. Continue row by row until the entire surface of the pie is covered.

recipe continues

10. Gently press the edges to secure the tiles and run a paring knife around the edge of the pie to trim the excess into a clean edge.

11. Chill the entire pie in the freezer until the oven has come to temperature. The pie can be frozen solid before baking or simply chilled through, about 20 minutes.

12. Preheat the oven to 400°F. Line a rimmed baking sheet with parchment paper.

13. When the oven has come to temperature, place the chilled pie on the prepared baking sheet. Bake for 25 minutes, then rotate the pie 180 degrees and lower the oven temperature to 350°F. If the edges are already brown, cover with a shield. Continue baking until the crust tiles look baked through in the center, checking every 30 minutes to rotate the pie and cover lightly with foil as necessary, 50 to 75 total minutes. (If baking from frozen, add 30 to 45 minutes to the bake time.)

14. Cool the pie slightly on a rack before slicing and serving.

SUGGESTED SUBSTITUTIONS

Dough alternatives: Basic (page 134), Spinach (page 162), Spinach with poppy seeds (page 162), Whole Wheat Cheddar Chive (page 165)

NOTES

If using sun-dried tomatoes packed in oil, make sure they are drained.

Baked surplus herb tiles make excellent crackers (see page 130).

FLORAL OF THE STORY

In 1901, my great-grandfather sailed to San Francisco from China in search of opportunities to better support his family. But he was unable to find work in California due to the racist climate of the time. According to family legend, he then rode a donkey down through Mexico, Guatemala, and El Salvador, ultimately settling in Tegucigalpa, Honduras.

He learned Spanish, adopted the name Joaquín Salvador, and opened up a general store that became so reputable patrons in the neighborhood would bring their money to stash in his establishment because they trusted him more than the local banks. Eventually, he sent for my great-grandmother and grandfather to join him in Honduras, cementing my family's history in the country for generations to come.

It is customary in Chinese culture to pay respects to the deceased, and my family honors this tradition with weekly visits to the gravesites of my great-grandparents and grandfather. These visits include tidying up the tombstones and refreshing the plots with bright new flower arrangements. Because of these rituals, fresh florals always make me contemplative about my family's past and my roots.

It may seem a bit macabre to mention these practices, especially in a cookbook, but as I wrap this undertaking, I can't help but reflect on all the steps so many people have taken over time that have led me here. My family has had an incredible impact on my formation. This exploration of food and feeding others, of risk-taking, and of thrilling in the unorthodox is attributable to their insatiable appetite for adventure and the ways they have empowered me to make this new living. This pie bouquet honors their legacy.

2 disks Basic Pie Dough (page 134)

MISO CARAMEL

1 cup (198 grams) granulated sugar

½ cup (118 milliliters) heavy cream

2 tablespoons (36 grams) white miso

PEAR FILLING

2½ pounds (1.1 kg) firm, ripe Bosc pears (about 5 large pears)

¼ cup (50 grams) granulated sugar

1. To make the miso caramel, combine the sugar and ¼ cup (59 milliliters) water in a 2-quart saucepan, stirring gently to wet the sugar. Bring to a boil and do not stir or agitate further.

2. When the sugar mixture reaches 260°F, about 8 minutes, remove from the heat and pour in the heavy cream. Return to low heat if the mixture seizes; otherwise whisk to combine. Add the miso and whisk until smooth.

3. Let cool completely before using in the pie filling. The miso caramel can be made ahead and stored in the refrigerator until use.

4. Remove any leaves or green backs on the flowers to ensure the blooms lay flat on the dough. Any flower parts that stick up will be subject to burning when the pie is baked. Depending on the size of the flower, petals can be gently plucked to be used individually.

recipe continues

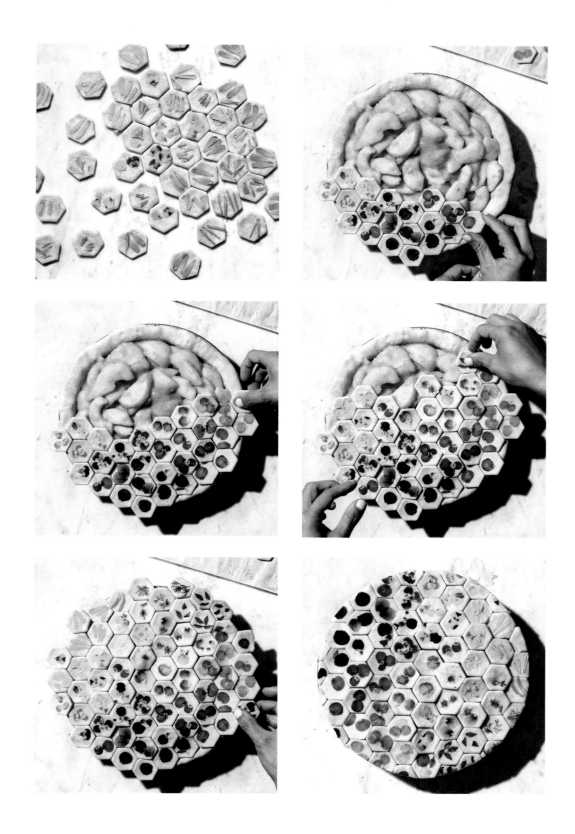

½ teaspoon ground cinnamon

¼ cup (28 grams) tapioca starch

1 teaspoon kosher salt

FLOWER TILE DESIGN NEEDS

15 to 20 assorted small edible flowers, such as pansies, nasturtiums, calendula, and borage (see page 14)

Parchment paper

1-inch hexagon cutter

Small bowl of water

Pastry brush

Paring knife

5. On a floured surface, roll one disk of dough into a 13-inch circle. Roll the dough onto the rolling pin and unfurl it onto a sheet of parchment paper.

6. Lightly brush a small section of the dough with water and apply a flower or small grouping of petals to the dough. Encircle the flower or petals on the dough with a 1-inch hexagonal cutter and punch out a floral dough tile, transferring it to a sheet of parchment. Continue applying flowers and cutting tiles until you have at least 70 tiles or have used up as much of the rolled dough as possible.

7. Place the tiles in the refrigerator to keep cool while preparing the filling. If you plan to chill the tiles for longer than 1 hour, cover the baking sheet to prevent the dough from drying out.

8. Roll the second disk of dough into a 14-inch circle. Roll the dough onto the rolling pin and unfurl it over a 9-inch pie pan. Taking the edges of the dough, gently ease the dough into the pan, nestling it into the inner elbows of the pie pan. Trim the excess dough with kitchen shears to create a 1-inch overhang. Fold the overhang back under, creating an elevated edge.

9. To prepare the pear filling, peel, core, and cut the pears into ¼-inch slices. Combine the pears, sugar, cinnamon, tapioca starch, and salt in a large bowl and gently fold to coat the fruit.

10. Fill the bottom of the pie shell with two layers of pear slices fitted closely together. Continue layering slices around the edges, going three-quarters of the way up the pie shell sides, leaving a well in the center. Pour 1 heaping cup (300 grams) of the cooled miso caramel into the well and fill the pie shell with the remaining pear slices, doming the fruit slightly in the center.

11. Remove the flower tiles from the refrigerator. Lightly brush water around the pie shell edge to secure the tiles. Fit the tiles closely together on the surface until the pie is fully covered, grouping flowers by color or arranging in a random pattern. Run a paring knife around the edge of the pie to trim the excess dough.

recipe continues

PIE DESIGNS

12. Chill the entire pie in the freezer until the oven has come to temperature. The pie can be frozen solid before baking or simply chilled through, about 20 minutes.

13. Preheat the oven to 400°F. Line a rimmed baking sheet with parchment.

14. When the oven has reached temperature, remove the pie from the freezer and place it on the prepared baking sheet. Bake the pie for 25 minutes, then rotate the pie 180 degrees and lower the oven temperature to 350°F. Cover the edges with a shield and lay a sheet of foil lightly on top to keep the flowers from singeing. Continue baking until the crust tiles look baked through, checking every 30 minutes to rotate the pie, 80 to 100 total minutes. (If baking from frozen, add 30 to 45 minutes to the bake time.) Remove the sheet of foil during the last 10 to 15 minutes of baking.

15. Cool the pie completely on a rack before slicing and serving.

SUGGESTED SUBSTITUTIONS

Dough alternatives: Beet (page 138), Black Sesame (page 141), Blueberry (page 144), Butterfly Pea Flower (page 147), Carrot (page 150), Cornflower (page 152), Dragon Fruit (page 155)

ACKNOWLEDGMENTS

Okay, let's be real. As someone with no professional culinary training, no prior publishing experience, and above-average anxiety, the process of writing this book was fraught with self-doubt and panic attacks. There were many days when I was dubious I'd survive to present the world with a finished product I am this proud of. And yet, here we are!

I owe so many thanks to everyone who walked with me, patiently held my hand, cheered me on, and/or fed me pizza. (And on that note, a shout-out to pizza, the *other* pie, for keeping me physically alive this year. You're the real MVP.) This undertaking was made possible by a wealth of people with a wealth of superpowers. Adequate words of gratitude evade me. Here's an incomprehensive but earnest attempt anyway.

Katherine Latshaw, my badass agent, you are hot pink in a world of grays and beiges. I love having you in my corner. Thanks for flinging open the doors for this project. I still can't believe the offer in that final email wasn't a typo.

Cassie Jones, my superlative editor, and Jill Zimmerman, you're the equivalent of hitting the jackpot. I want to frame your collective tracked Word document giggles. Thank you for humoring me and turning this into something that's so much more than pies and puns. And one million high fives to the whole William Morrow/HarperCollins crew for handling this package with so much care.

Photographer Ed Anderson and food stylist Olivia Caminiti, the two weeks we spent together were some kind of magical dream. Thank you for bringing these pies and tarts exuberantly to life while also being the most chill and laid-back team of all time.

Tammy Hui, Julia Boulos, Michelle Moo, Grace Wang, Dr. Timothy Eugene, thank you for your dedication and diligence. May you and your loved ones live to tolerate the sight of butter again.

Oliva Church, you appeared on the scene like a dairy godmother. I'm grateful for your butter flattening prowess.

Jessica Huang, I occasionally flip through the proposal you beautified and it's all the heart eyes every time. You've got deft design skillz with a z.

Nirvana Habash, you are the ultimate hypequeen. I'll never forget when I was writing this proposal and feeling completely out of my league. Your pep talk stuck with me the entire book writing process, and I'm beyond grateful. Everyone should be so lucky to have a friend like you.

High Point Public Library, thank you for being a free, well-lit space where people can read, write, and escape all the snacks that taunt them at home.

Popo, usted siempre ha sido y sigue siendo mi ídola. Gracias por darme esta vida comedera, llena de amor y estándares altos. Mami, you shaped Wingaling and me with a lifetime of the best home-cooked and home-baked fare. Thanks for letting me hold the mixer from the very beginning. Papa, you are truly the best person I know and your unconditional enthusiasm for food is a light in my life. Geoffrey, you will always be the top baker in this family. Casa Quan, Hui family, and Ko family, what great fortune to have you as my people.

Santi ponti, your blissful snores were a soothing complement to my kitchen chaos this year. Thank you for dutifully hoovering up the crumbs when I was too exhausted to vacuum.

Ben, you schlepped so many groceries, washed so many dishes, and managed so many of my emails for this book specifically, I consider you second author. Thank you for jumping into this wild venture with me. Tomato.

My Instagram zealots, look what happens when you make all hell bake loose! Thank you for loving modern geometric pies so furiously that it completely transformed my life. You encrusted me with the opportunity to explore this intersection of art, design, baking, and feeding people, and it's been a wild ride. You have my whole tart.

And to the haters, #thisiswhatitlookslikebaked.

UNIVERSAL CONVERSION CHART

OVEN TEMPERATURE EQUIVALENTS

250°F = 120°C

275°F = 135°C

300°F = 150°C

325°F = 160°C

350°F = 180°C

375°F = 190°C

400°F = 200°C

425°F = 220°C

450°F = 230°C

475°F = 240°C

500°F = 260°C

MEASUREMENT EQUIVALENTS

Measurements should always be level unless directed otherwise.

⅛ teaspoon = 0.5 mL

¼ teaspoon = 1 mL

½ teaspoon = 2 mL

1 teaspoon = 5 mL

1 tablespoon = 3 teaspoons = ½ fluid ounce = 15 mL

2 tablespoons = ⅛ cup = 1 fluid ounce = 30 mL

4 tablespoons = ¼ cup = 2 fluid ounces = 60 mL

5⅓ tablespoons = ⅓ cup = 3 fluid ounces = 80 mL

8 tablespoons = ½ cup = 4 fluid ounces = 120 mL

10⅔ tablespoons = ⅔ cup = 5 fluid ounces = 160 mL

12 tablespoons = ¾ cup = 6 fluid ounces = 180 mL

16 tablespoons = 1 cup = 8 fluid ounces = 240 mL

INDEX

NOTE: Page references in *italics* indicate recipe photographs.

HarperCollins books may be purchased for educational,
business, or sales promotional use. For information, please email
the Special Markets Department at SPsales@harpercollins.com.

FIRST EDITION

DESIGNED BY RENATA DE OLIVEIRA
PHOTOGRAPHY BY ED ANDERSON

Geometric backgrounds by Shutterstock

Library of Congress Cataloging-in-Publication Data
has been applied for.

ISBN 978-0-06-291122-3

20 21 22 23   TC   10 9 8 7 6 5 4 3 2 1